# THE SECRETS OF A SUCCESSFUL READING GROUP

- The six discussion topics that get the most out of a book

- The one essential requirement for "couples only" groups

- The shortcomings of "theme" choices for books ... and some intriguing suggestions from groups that made them work

- The "magic number" of members for great discussions

- What types of books to pick **besides** novels

- Wonderful sources for book titles—from lesser-known serious books to some "sleepers" read by intellectual celebrities

- The book category that **never** works in a reading group (no kidding!)

## THE READING GROUP BOOK

**David Laskin,** a freelance writer, is the author of numerous books, as well as a contributor to such publications as *Family Life, The New York Times,* and *Esquire.* He lives in Seattle.

**Holly Hughes,** freelance writer and editor, is a contributing editor to *Literary Cavalcade* magazine. She lives in New York City. The authors were members of the same reading group for 14 years.

# THE READING GROUP BOOK

The Complete Guide to
Starting and Sustaining a Reading Group,
with Annotated Lists of 250 Titles
for Provocative Discussion

## David Laskin
### and
## Holly Hughes

A PLUME BOOK

PLUME
Published by the Penguin Group
Penguin Books USA Inc., 375 Hudson Street,
New York, New York 10014, U.S.A.
Penguin Books Ltd, 27 Wrights Lane, London W8 5TZ, England
Penguin Books Australia Ltd, Ringwood, Victoria, Australia
Penguin Books Canada Ltd, 10 Alcorn Avenue,
Toronto, Ontario, Canada M4V 3B2
Penguin Books (N.Z.) Ltd, 182-190 Wairau Road,
Auckland 10, New Zealand

Penguin Books Ltd, Registered Offices:
Harmondsworth, Middlesex, England

First published by Plume, an imprint of Dutton Signet,
a division of Penguin Books USA Inc.

First Printing, February, 1995
10  9  8  7  6  5  4

 REGISTERED TRADEMARK—MARCA REGISTRADA

LIBRARY OF CONGRESS CATALOGING-IN-PUBLICATION DATA

Laskin, David.
    The reading group book: the complete guide to starting and sustaining
a reading group, with annotated lists of 250 titles for provocative discussion / David Laskin and Holly Hughes.
        p.  cm.
    Includes bibliographical references.
    ISBN 0-452-27201-7
    1. Group reading—United States.  I. Hughes, Holly.  II. Title.
LC6615.L37  1995
374.22—dc20                                                      94-30200
                                                                     CIP

Printed in the United States of America
Set in Garamond Light
Designed by Eve L. Kirch

BOOKS ARE AVAILABLE AT QUANTITY DISCOUNTS WHEN USED TO PROMOTE PRODUCTS OR
SERVICES. FOR INFORMATION PLEASE WRITE TO PREMIUM MARKETING DIVISION, PENGUIN
BOOKS USA INC., 375 HUDSON STREET, NEW YORK, NY 10014.

To the members of our original
New York City reading group

# Acknowledgments

Our first and biggest thanks go to the book group members all over the country who shared their wisdom, anecdotes, advice, contacts, and most of all their favorite book titles with us. This book would not have been possible without their help.

We are also indebted to the bookstore owners and employees who talked with us about their experiences with book groups and who helped put us in touch with group members: Virginia Vallentine at Denver's Tattered Cover, Jim Harris at Prairie Lights Books in Iowa City, Vivien Jennings of Rainy Day Books in Fairway, Missouri, Kate Williams at the Barnes & Noble in Fresno, California, Kristen Kennell at Elliott Bay Books in Seattle, Felice Rose at New York City's Shakespeare & Company, and Jill Dunbar at Three Lives bookstore, also in New York City. Christy Wiencke, who writes the *Reading Women* newsletter, gave freely of her time and her knowledge of what groups are reading and why.

Elizabeth Long, a sociologist at Rice University, provided invaluable help in organizing and researching the chapter on the history of book groups and shared her thoughts on the role that these groups have played over the years in the social and intellectual lives of members.

Lonnie Plecha, senior editor of the Great Books Foundation, answered questions about the history of the Great Books movement and explained how the organization works today.

Our editor, Deb Brody, was a dream to work with from start to finish. And our agent, Diane Cleaver, was, as always, insightful, tireless, and gracefully efficient.

Special thanks also go to Nancy Bradgon of Portland Arts and Lectures, Jack Litewka and Jane Ellis, Liza Kennedy, and to Joe Esposito and to Joelle Delbourgo for suggesting that we write this book in the first place.

Between the two of us, we have now participated in four different book groups going back fourteen years. What we learned by talking about books each month with our fellow members has been the most enjoyable, and most essential, part of our research for this book.

# Contents

# Introduction

For fourteen years, our reading group was a polestar in both our lives. The seven original members, plus three delightful later additions, went through a lot in those years—one divorce, one separation-and-reconciliation, three marriages, the birth of six children and the death of one, seven apartment moves, three apartment renovations, four relocations out of the city, at least a dozen job changes, one retirement, and the deaths of three dogs.

We met faithfully nearly every month for those fourteen years, barring the occasional August lapse, though everybody didn't always make it to every meeting—or, as was the case with some, came often without having read much of the book.

Over the years, naturally, book discussion took up less of the evening, as we got to know each other better and better and spent a significant part of each meeting night telling one another what had gone on in our lives in the intervening month. We say this, but then remember that some of our liveliest and most intense book discussions happened in the last few meetings, sometimes with only three or four people there. It all depended on the book.

We still aren't quite sure why the group lost its will to live. We were scheduled to read *Women in Love* one month, and no one ended up making it to the meeting. Half-hearted attempts were made to schedule another date, but everyone canceled for that second meeting too. It seemed fruitless to reschedule, and without saying anything formal to one another, we all threw in the towel.

But we still miss the group. We miss hearing about Adele's wonderful garden (and sitting in the garden on our annual weekend retreats to her house in upstate New York!). We miss seeing one another's kids grow up and petting each other's dogs. We miss getting movie recommendations from each other, and finding out what was worth reading in *The New Yorker* or *Vanity Fair*. We miss the lively, often surprising book discussions and the occasional all-out debates we used to have.

In a sense, this book grew directly out of the rise and fall of our reading group—as a way to celebrate it and to understand why this informal institution became such a force in our lives. Over the years, whenever we mentioned our group to friends, relatives, or colleagues, we often found ourselves bombarded by questions: Whose idea was this? How did you get it going? How do you decide what to read? What do you talk about each time? How can I start one of my own? Our primary goal in *The Reading Group Book* is to answer these questions: to provide all the information book lovers need to start their own group or, if they're already in a group, to keep it going strong.

This is, above all, a practical book of information. We tell how book discussion groups have changed over the years, from Anne Hutchinson's sermon analysis circle in Puritan New England to Barbra Streisand's Hollywood book club. We describe how to start a group—how to give it focus as well as how to set up ground rules for choosing a book and scheduling meetings. We'll give you ideas on what kinds of food and drink to serve at your meetings. We offer pointers on getting a lively discussion going. We'll help you resolve the problems that are most likely to derail your book group—poor attendance, difficulty in choosing a book, and members who fail to finish reading the book.

Since the choice of what book to discuss is the single most important factor in a successful reading group meeting, a major section of our book is devoted to reading lists. We'll tell you about books that we know are both readable and worth discussing. We have carefully annotated our book lists so that you can get some idea of what each book is really like, and what kinds of issues are likely to crop up in your discussions. When people who belong to different reading groups meet, they invariably compare notes on what books have worked well for their group and why. This word-of-mouth grapevine has made America's book groups into a kind of underground movement or subculture: there are definitely "hot" book group books, and they aren't by any means your typical bestsellers or canonized classics.

When we started in on our research, we wanted to contact as many groups around the country as we could. So we used the same technique that many book groups rely on for finding members and swapping book titles: we networked. The result was astonishing. Far from having to hunt for book groups, we found them everywhere we turned—every time we mentioned to someone that we were doing this book, at a wedding, at a holiday party, in the playground, someone gave us another name to call. And every group we talked to was somehow unique and taught us something new.

We contacted groups of women who had been reading together since the late 1950s and had seen one another's children grow up, go to college, and start book groups of their own. We found radical lesbian groups and suburban couples groups. There were men-only groups that went to ballgames together and women-only groups that went to Mexico together. Groups of engineers. Writers' groups. Neighborhood groups. Some groups had even given themselves names: The We of the Never Never, The Group That Has Affairs, Queen for a Month, The Harpies, and The Goddesses, to name some of the more eccentric ones.

Some members refer to their group as a book club, others say book group, still others reading group (as we did). We use the terms interchangeably throughout.

The number and variety of groups is infinite, as far as we can tell. Our research yielded few hard facts or statistics—informal, voluntary clubs like these don't get counted in official censuses. But we have been able to draw some tentative conclusions from our random sampling.

We were struck most of all by how similar the goals and motives of book group members are. "The more your work life goes on, the more you think, 'What happened to all those great books I used to read?' " one woman tells us, articulating the thoughts of many.

"It's really important to me to discuss what I read with other people," another member says. "I read things my husband would not consider. The more I read and the older I get, the more questions I have—and the more I want to discuss these questions."

Someone else puts it this way: "I joined a group because I was always reading books and thinking, 'There's a lot going on here—I wish I knew what the hell it was. I really wish I had someone to discuss it with.' " We heard this same idea voiced from New York City to Seattle, Los Angeles to Houston, Boston to Denver—and lots of smaller towns in between.

"People are so tired of trivial conversations," says Vivien Jennings, president of Rainy Day Books in Kansas City and the leader of a book group of mothers and daughters and daughters-in-law. "We don't just want to talk about business and sports and kids anymore. We want to talk about subjects that make our brains feel alive. I think this accounts for the popularity of the groups now. Also, people would rather go to a book group than go to a bar or stay home and watch TV. In a way, the groups act as surrogate neighborhoods and families. They connect interesting people to each other."

Reading groups answer a need for intelligent conversation. They provide a way to exchange ideas, engage in debate, and share rapturous insights. As Elizabeth Long, a sociologist at Rice University in Houston, Texas, who has been studying book groups, puts it, "People value their book groups because they love having a group of people they can talk about ideas with. They get to discuss topics they might not discuss otherwise—issues of morality, politics, ecology. Thoughts on books are enriched by having other people's lives to draw on. We just don't have a lot of other outlets for this in our culture."

We couldn't think of *any* other outlets—not work, not marriage, not friendship (although friends do sometimes exchange books). Not even educational institutions; perhaps these least of all. We were struck by how many reading group members mentioned how different their college classes were from the discussions in their groups. College experiences seem to be much on the minds of people in reading groups. They'll tell you what their college majors were right off the bat—even though it isn't relevant and probably hasn't been relevant for years. Maybe it's because book groups at their best are a bit like school without teachers, tests, or term papers—a kind of dream classroom where you can sip wine and nibble snacks, where it's perfectly acceptable to say that you adored a character in a novel because she reminded you of your sister, where no one looks down their nose at you if you declare, "Stream of consciousness? Nah, this is just sloppy writing."

Thinking back over their group's history together, people tell us that their most memorable meetings were their most heated, most impassioned: the time when Sue thought Joanne's reaction to *The Remains of the Day* was too callous; when Tom insisted that Virginia Woolf was the most overrated novelist in the language; when Gillian accused Cormac McCarthy of "pornography of violence." And just about every group we talked to has had an unforgettable meeting in which the book was a springboard for a wider-range discussion—about race relations, religion, sex, or some other topic that they wandered into because they had all read this particular book together. The point is, anything goes—and often, the more contentious the better.

Many of the groups we contacted had been together a long time—ten or twenty years—and had been through a lot together. Their book choices changed, sometimes radically, over the years—from Germaine Greer and Malcolm X in the sixties to Robert Bly and Jane Smiley in the nineties. But even more significant, their emotional bonds grew stronger and deeper through the years.

"We see our group as a safe place," one member of an all-women group in Seattle notes. "We are a tight group of women, and we feel we can say anything to one another. Events have drawn us together. There was a horrible murder in the neighborhood and the group was a real source of support during this time. When someone gets sick we bring each other dinner. We're good at crisis management. For some of us, the group is the one consistent element in our lives."

Vicki says that the women in her group have "dealt with a whole lot of things" in the twenty-six years they have been together: one member died in a car accident; the husband of another was shot to death; there have been divorces and remarriages; the group endured the Vietnam era and together struggled through the first wave of the women's movement. Most of the women were at-home moms when the group began, and the group was their sole escape from home and children. Now that their children are grown, most have careers of their own. Often the members of this group don't see each other outside of the monthly book group meetings. They do not consider all the other members close friends, but these women do have a strong sense of solidarity. They are involved with one another; they cherish and rely on this involvement.

We heard variations on this theme time and again. Just as reading group discussions strike a balance between the academic and the personal, so group relationships occupy a rare middle ground between the intimate and the intellectual. As members exchange ideas about which they care deeply, they get to know one another's minds inside and out—sometimes far better than friends or spouses do. For Larry, his all-male group became especially important when he was going through a rough personal time: "My marriage broke up at the same time that my career fell apart. I valued my book group at this time, not because I was interested in laying my soul bare or getting a therapy session. Instead I wanted to demonstrate to myself my ability to bring intellectual energy to bear and take my mind off personal problems. The group was a help."

Chris describes his book group this way: "I know far more about my fellow group members than I would have had I met them at a series of parties. At parties you'd hear about someone's career and family. But at the book group I know what they think and what they're passionate about. You get so little of this in standard social engagement. That's why a book club is so valuable."

"In my group I feel so strongly about what we're discussing that I will say things about myself that I would never say in another setting," one woman reports. "When we're talking about Alice Walker or Margaret Atwood or Jane Smiley, I'll say, 'This happened to me. I've been there.' I've been amazed at the things that we all share. But the wonderful thing is, you never feel it will be used against you. You never feel threatened."

Let's not forget about the pleasure principle either: the sheer joy of reading wonderful books and discussing them with like-minded people. "In the group I'm in now, it almost doesn't matter what we read, we always have really good discussions," one woman says. "The pleasure of reading and talking about books is what makes it work. There is something about reading these books and sharing them with other people that makes me feel rich."

Or as another member puts it so succinctly, "It's been one of my mainstay social things, it's very stimulating, and it means I always have something to read."

Jim Harris, who owns Prairie Lights bookstore in Iowa City, stays in touch with scores of local book groups, suggesting titles, keeping them up-to-date on hot new books. We asked him, as we asked book store managers and book group members all over the country, why he thought the groups had really taken off in the past decade or so. "The answer is simple," he replies. "People join these groups because they like to talk about books. To read and discuss. When you get right down to it, there's no difference between a reading group and a bowling group. We just hope they don't end up throwing bowling balls at each other."

We heard lots of different takes on this issue, but this was our favorite. To read and discuss. We like to think of our book as a kind of marriage manual dedicated to the happy union of these two activities.

# 1

# A Brief History of the Reading Group in America

When the two of us were invited to join a New York City book group back in the late 1970s, we were both intrigued—and also a little dubious about the whole enterprise. We were vaguely aware that other people in odd corners of the city were getting together in the evenings to talk about books. There was a faint buzz about the idea in the air, but we hesitated before committing ourselves. The whole concept of a book group seemed awfully trendy; the word "group" alone had suspect vibes—it sounded like support group, group therapy, recovery group, group dynamics. *My book group.* It was so . . . well, so seventies.

Just shows how ignorant *we* were. Far from being a newly hatched fad, book groups have actually been around in one form or another since the dawn of American history. What's even more surprising, the reasons why people join book clubs have stayed pretty much the same through the centuries. The book group buzz that we first picked up back in the seventies has grown a good deal louder since then, but it's just the latest variation on a very old theme: a grass-roots kind of literary pursuit that's totally in keeping with such all-American traits as a love of freedom, an envious disdain for Old World culture, and a yen for self-improvement.

No less a figure than the noted Puritan religious leader Anne Hutchinson is credited with forming America's first literary discussion group. It may even have started before she hit these shores; while sailing from England to the Massachusetts Bay Colony in 1634, she supposedly gathered her fellow female passengers each week to talk about that Sunday's sermon. And once she had established herself in Boston, Hutchinson invited interested women to her parlor twice each week for sermon discussions. The group swiftly progressed from literary analysis to theological disputation—and just as swiftly ran afoul of the male Puritan establishment. The authorities accused Hutchinson of "troubling the peace of the commonwealth" and "maintaining a meeting and an assembly in your house that hath been condemned by the general assembly as a thing not tolerable nor comely in the sight of God nor fitting for your sex." For these transgressions, Anne Hutchinson was banished. (Remember *that* the next time discussion in your book group grows inflamed.)

Theodora Penny Martin in *The Sound of Our Own Voice,* her history of women's study clubs in America, points out that Anne Hutchinson's group, short-lived as it was, set an important precedent for the literary clubs that followed: it was all female; its goal was self-education; the leader was a strong-minded and magnetic individual; the tone was uplifting; and the focus of the discussions broadened out from literature to current events.

Other colonial-era book groups kept a considerably lower profile than the Anne Hutchinson circle. Respectable women at the time were expected to devote themselves to cooking, child-rearing, and homemaking, and church activities were the only sanctioned break from the domestic routine. And so, of necessity, women combined book discussion with church work. In the few scanty records that have survived, we learn of women's church groups reading and talking about religious works while they sewed quilts and samplers to sell at church bazaars. Gradually, the rigors of Puritanism relaxed a bit, and by the nineteenth century women who were interested in ideas were able to step out from under the umbrella of the church. As early as 1800, a book club met in Chelsea, Connecticut, determined to "enlighten the understanding and expand the ideas of its members." The books these women discussed included an early *History of Columbus,* George Frederic Watts's *Treatise of the Mind,* and Benjamin Trumbull's *Complete History of Connecticut.* Around the same time "reading parties" began cropping up in Boston. At these, a lecturer would be engaged to speak in someone's home, and afterwards guests lingered in the parlor to exchange ideas. Though most of the speakers were male, the audience was largely female, of that peculiar Boston breed known as the "bluestocking." (Henry James' 1886 novel *The Bostonians* is an unforgettable portrait of Boston's bluestocking society.) Elizabeth Peabody, a renowned Boston bluestocking of the day, had a bookshop at West Street and there, in the late 1840s, her fellow bluestocking Margaret Fuller gathered women for "Conversations" on literature and culture. (These "in-store" book groups were the forerunners of the groups that meet today in the gleaming new "super stores" that Barnes & Noble and Borders Books are opening in upscale urban neighborhoods.)

Also among the reading group pioneers were freed African-American women living in eastern cities in the early 1830s. Having suffered the deprivations of slavery, these women were determined to acquire an education, and they promptly discovered they'd have to do it themselves. Book groups served as their informal classrooms.

White women in the Midwest began clubbing together for much the same reason. A group formed in Rochester, Michigan, in 1847 to read and discuss their own original compositions. In New Harmony, Indiana, a Minerva Society formed in 1859 for the purpose of female self-improvement; its founder was Constance Owen Fauntleroy, the granddaughter of utopian philosopher Robert Owen, the man who had founded the town, and she ran it according to strict parliamentary procedure. The members gathered to debate contemporary issues (for example, "Do Facts or Fiction Contribute Most to Mental Enjoyment?") and to discuss compositions and poems, many of which were their own original work. They even collaborated on writing a short novel, with each member contributing a chapter.

These antebellum groups were for the most part isolated, local flowerings—little oases of culture and self-education scattered widely in the vast cultural desert of America's hinterlands. But after the Civil War, a mass movement of women's study clubs swept through the nation at large. Helen Hooven Santmyer's 1982 best-seller . . . And Ladies of the Club chronicles several decades in the life of one such group, formed in 1868 in a small mid-Ohio town. As one historian of the period describes it, the spontaneous proliferation of these clubs in the 1870s was like "some very contagious virus" let loose in the female population. Women club members had no idea that their peers in other parts of the country were doing the same thing in the same way for the same reasons: it was a true craze, like the rock 'n' roll mania of the 1950s, only this one spread all on its own, without being fueled by any mass media.

Two very high-profile clubs of the period were Sorosis (what an unfortunate name!), founded by journalist Jane Cunningham Croly in New York City in 1868, and the New England Woman's Club (NEWC), which got going the same year in Boston. Croly wrote that she hoped that by banding together in a study club women would be "seized by the divine spirit of inquiry and aspiration" and caught up in "the thought and progress of the age." Sorosis women were for the most part professionals—artists, poets, editors, historians, and doctors—and quite daring for the time. Rather than meet in one another's parlors, which would have been the nice conventional thing to do, they gathered twice each month on Mondays at the fashionable restaurant Delmonico's, until then the exclusive domain of men and their female companions. Sorosis ran, like a university, from September to June. Generally, a meeting began with the presentation of a paper, and then discussion of the issues would follow. The NEWC members, though just as high-minded as their counterparts in Sorosis, were more traditional in their daily pursuits: few had independent paid careers, though many worked hard as volunteers for charities and social improvement.

Male Boston intellectuals such as Bronson Alcott (Louisa May Alcott's father), Henry James (the novelist's father), and Ralph Waldo Emerson applauded the NEWC, but in New York the press ridiculed Sorosis as a bunch of self-centered bluestockings. If women insisted on getting up these silly little clubs, the New York literary establishment argued, at least they should perform some useful task like knitting socks. But for women to meet *in public* for the sole purpose of intellectual "inquiry and aspiration" was unsupportable.

Croly, however, was not one to take an attack lying down. "Suppose . . . that some of us did begin to realize that we were growing more and more stupid, and more and more 'dull,' and more and more 'inane' every day," she wrote in defense of the group, "and determined to do something to help ourselves, and that something was Sorosis, would not even that be accomplishing a little?" More than a century later, several of the individuals we interviewed for this book agreed, in different words, that they too had joined a book group in order to ward off stupidity, dullness, and inanity. Jane Croly was definitely onto something.

Sorosis and the NEWC inspired a host of followers in other cities around the nation, but many other literary clubs sprang up with no knowledge of what was happening in New York and Boston. From the 1870s through the 1890s, these clubs were all the rage all over the country. Any town worthy of the name had its Shakespeare Club or Browning Society or Literary Delvers. Clubs printed up programs, invited speakers, devised lofty mottos such as "Knowledge is the treasure of which study is the key" or "Live with great minds and you will learn to think." The Rhode Island Woman's Club had amassed 200 members by 1889. The Mother's Club of Cambridge (Massachusetts) combined discussion of child-rearing techniques with literary analysis. From El Paso, Texas, to Caribou, Maine, from Elmira, New York, to Madison, Indiana, women were gathering on weekday afternoons to discuss American and English literature (the Brownings, George Eliot, and John Stuart Mill were favorites) as well as the masterpieces of classical antiquity. They also debated burning issues of the day, such as socialism, the Russian political system, the tariff.

By and large, though, club women preferred to look back at the monuments of the past rather than at the new works and ideas that were sweeping through art, literature, and science. As one historian notes, the groups took little notice of Freud or Darwin, and they showed no sign of being aware that impressionism was revolutionizing painting and naturalism changing the novel in their own time. The plays of Ibsen and Edward Bellamy's *Looking Backward: 2000–1887* were about as daring and "modern" as they ever got.

At most clubs, dues were collected to pay for printed programs, reports, ballots, and maybe flowers, postage, and refreshments. Meetings generally lasted about two hours and usually took place during the day on weekdays—never on Sunday and rarely at night, since a woman was still not supposed to be seen outside her home after dark unless escorted by a man (and men were firmly barred from these gatherings). Roll call was taken as the meetings came to order; members were fined for absences.

In one group women responded to the roll call with quotations from Shakespeare. We couldn't resist speculating about which passages the ladies might have selected.

"Mrs. Dexter?"

"O! that this too, too solid flesh would melt."

"Mrs. Renfew?"

"Sicklied o'er by the pale cast of thought."

"Mrs. Henderson?"

"Age cannot wither her nor custom stale her infinite variety."

Then as now, club members had to resist the temptation to let the meetings degenerate into chitchat and gossip. As one nineteenth-century woman admitted, "There is still truth in the satirical remark that the subject of conversation at our teas is 'first Shelley, then Charley, then Mary Ann.' " In some cities women jockeyed for admission to the "right" clubs, and once they were in, they flaunted their new culture as yet another prestigious acquisiton. Edith Wharton—who was always pretty scornful of women's causes and the pushy, inelegant women who espoused them—satirized the female culture craze in her 1911 short story "Xingu," which begins:

> Mrs. Ballinger is one of the ladies who pursue Culture in bands, as though it were dangerous to meet it alone. To this end she had founded the Lunch Club, an association of herself and several other indomitable huntresses of erudition.

Study club historian Theodora Martin admits that these culture clubs of the nineteenth century may indeed have been silly, shallow, and affected at times, but she adds that it is certainly unfair to dismiss the entire movement as a fashionable fad. Many women spoke glowingly of how much real learning and pleasure they got out of their clubs, and how eagerly they anticipated the meetings. "To some of us, it has at times afforded our only relaxation from daily routine outside of our church life," wrote Mrs. Reuben Kellogg of the Sorosis of Elmira, New York. And Sallie Southall Cotten of North Carolina noted in 1884 that she joined the literary club "So I would feel *obliged* to read books which otherwise I would neglect"—

another sentiment that we have heard again and again from contemporary members.

Sociologist Elizabeth Long attributes the sudden rise of these study and literary clubs in the late nineteenth century to women's "extraordinary hunger for knowledge." "Women at the time did not have higher education open to them," she told us, "and they hungered to be taken seriously and to acquire cultural authority." The only way to satisfy this hunger was to take matters into their own hands. As Theodora Martin also points out, middle-class women had a good deal more time and energy to read and meet after the Civil War due to such labor-saving innovations as indoor plumbing, home canning, department stores, and factory-made bread, beer, and soap. The sharp drop in the birth rate (from 7 children per family in 1800 to 4.24 per family in 1880) also freed up women. There are no hard statistics documenting exactly how many women belonged to these clubs in the late nineteenth century, but we do know that by 1906, no less than 5,000 local organizations had joined the General Federation of Women's Clubs, and this was estimated to represent only 5 to 10 percent of total clubs.

By the time these figures were gathered, most of the women's literary clubs had substantially altered their original purpose and focus. Clubs that had been meeting for ten or twenty years to discuss books and ideas began to turn their attention to social and political issues—summer schools and parks for local children, the conditions of tenement apartment houses, the education of immigrants, women's suffrage, and prohibition. After the turn of the century, notes Martin, the clubs turned from the "realm of abstract thought" to "education for service": "These new club women moved quickly and efficiently from philosophy to philanthropy and rarely looked back." The skills that club members had developed—public speaking, debate, research, and literary analysis—came in handy in dealing with government bureaucrats, hospital boards, and school officials. And so the first great upsurge of

book groups came to an end, not because interest had pe-
tered out, but because the members had changed their focus
and direction.

The impulse to form book discussion groups did not die
out completely—a May 1929 issue of *Scribner's Magazine,* for
example, ran an outline for forming literary clubs—but it did
go dormant for several decades. As Elizabeth Long puts it,
"There is more continuity from old to new than one might
imagine. A lot of clubs today come from organizations like so-
rorities, the American Association of University Women, the
League of Women Voters, and the like. These are modern versions of the older women's organizations. The notion of book
clubs has been passed down through generations of women."
Long points to several book clubs in the Houston and Austin
areas that have been in existence for well over a century. A
couple of the groups that we interviewed, too, were founded
during this first flush of book clubs and have been going
strong ever since. We heard of one group, for example, called
The Ingleside, that began in the college town of Indiana,
Pennsylvania, back in 1882 for the purpose of "mutual improvement and social enjoyment," as its official rules state,
and that is sustained today by the great- and great-great-
grandchildren of the founders. In the early days the members
reread all of Shakespeare and studied history and essays, but
gradually discussion began to revolve around "papers" written
by members and read at the meetings. Recent topics have
ranged from Stephen W. Hawking to Jules Verne, Saul Bellow,
rivers of the world, the 1939 World's Fair, Thomas Jeffer-
son, and Agatha Christie. "Some of us have difficulty to keep
from dozing through the paper following a virtual banquet
of a meal," confesses Elinor Gordon Blair, the great-
granddaughter-in-law of one of the founders, "but the papers
have been invariably excellent."

The next flowering of book clubs in America was the so-
called Great Books movement, which swept the country after

World War II. The idea behind the movement grew out of a course originally taught by Professor John Erskine at Columbia University in New York City, around the time of World War I. Erskine, convinced that increasing specialization of knowledge was cramping the liberal arts curriculum, assigned Columbia juniors and seniors readings in the great monuments of western literature and philosophy, from Homer to William James, and then led discussions of the texts. This concept—which, believe it or not, was considered a radical innovation at the time—was introduced to the University of Chicago in 1929 by its dynamic, dashing thirty-year-old president Robert M. Hutchins and his friend and colleague Mortimer J. Adler. Hutchins and Adler assembled a reading list similar to Erskine's for their course at Chicago, and they taught it initially as a small seminar, emphasizing group discussion—the more heated the better. The instant, huge popularity of this seminar sent shock waves rippling through the conservative educational establishment.

In time, Hutchins and Adler took their Great Books idea outside the confines of the university—first to high schools and then to adult groups meeting in libraries, gymnasiums, and churches. They received a surge of publicity when they put together a group of prominent Chicago businessmen bent on self-improvement—the so-called "Fat Man Group." The Fat Men loved the whole concept, even their nickname, and the gospel of the Great Books spread fast.

Hutchins and Adler's guiding principle was that the Great Books were totally accessible—that anyone willing to open his or her mind to these works could sit down and discuss them. To insure the books' accessibility, they arranged for the titles to be printed in cheap paperback editions. The Great Books concept really hit a nerve in the years following World War II. Returning GIs, housewives with a hunger for knowledge and intellectual companionship, white-collar workers who had never attended college, college graduates who had grown rusty, people who yearned to "better" themselves—all of these segments of the population formed the rank and file of the Great Books movement. The idea "swept the country as a cultural fashion attractive to people with no academic pretensions or aspirations but with much desire to be cultivated 'great bookies,' " writes James Sloan Allen in his book *The Romance of Commerce and Culture.*

By the end of 1946, 20,000 people were participating, and the following year an independent non-profit organization— the Great Books Foundation—was set up to administer the program, sell the books, and coordinate the groups. At its heyday in the late 1950s, the Great Books Foundation had registered 50,000 participants in 2,700 groups in America (with a few scattered overseas). And hundreds of other study groups were organized informally, through universities, libraries, civic organizations, and adult education programs. The Great Books movement was, in Allen's words, "the most ambitious program of adult education ever and the premier cultural event of postwar America."

The "curriculum" offered by the Great Books Foundation was essentially a hit parade of Dead White Males. Homer, Aeschylus, Sophocles, and Plato led off the list, and it continued down through the ages with Shakespeare, Swift, Montesquieu, Voltaire, Marx, Melville, Darwin, Dostoyevski, Mark Twain, William James, Tolstoy, and Henry Adams. No women. No people of color (with the exception of St. Augustine, who was born in Numidia, though most of his career was in Europe). No Native Americans or even South Americans. This was the canon of canons.

The Foundation, which is still going strong today, advises groups to have two leaders, or facilitators, whose role is to keep conversation moving briskly along the right track. The guiding principle is known as "shared inquiry"—the leaders toss out open-ended, provocative questions that get group members thinking and talking about the texts. The Foundation publishes "reader aids" with sample questions to assist and inspire leaders—for example, for Sophocles's *Oedipus the*

*King* the reader aid suggests questions such as: Does Oedipus deserve his fate? Does Oedipus represent the inevitable "fate" of parents and children? If you do not know that you are committing evil, have you committed it? Leaders are firmly discouraged from lecturing, and they aren't supposed to supply the answers to their questions. The Foundation even offers a brief, intensive training course at which leaders can master the art of shared inquiry. By and large, group leaders are not teachers or academics but rather individuals who want to make an extra commitment to their groups. To ensure continuity, the Great Books Foundation publishes guidelines and book lists, and helps people plug into ongoing groups or form groups of their own. As part of a package deal, groups can order their books directly from the Foundation.

At its peak in the late 1950s, the Great Books movement was studied by a team of sociologists from the National Opinion Research Center, who interviewed and sent questionnaires to 1,909 members around the country. The researchers found that people who signed up for the Great Books program tended to be "well-educated, high-status, socially active, youngish adults," neither "ivory-tower intellectuals" nor social misfits nor "climbers" but rather "middlebrow" people with "middle-class values and norms of community participation." Their reasons for joining a Great Books group included desire for knowledge and improved critical thinking, a need to broaden and improve oneself, an interest in becoming more deeply acquainted with "what the greatest minds in history have to say about the basic issues of life," and a desire to converse with like-minded people about ideas. The sociologists concluded that people joined the groups because they "were concerned about the intellectual narrowness of their lives and wanted not just knowledge of great authors but also contact with other group members who shared their intellectual orientations. It is the combination of the social and the intellectual—not one or the other—which appears to be the hallmark of the participants' motivations."

Sound familiar?

As the tranquilized 1950s gave way to the rebellious 1960s, the Great Books movement waned. Fewer people wanted to have their reading matter dictated from on high. The arbitrarily chosen list of past masterpieces was less and less relevant to people's lives. Basically, the format was too uptight—besides, more people had gone to college and gotten their fill of great books there. So even though the Great Books Foundation is still around, in the past couple of decades it has shifted its focus from adult book groups to its "junior program" for students in elementary, middle, and high schools. The junior program, often offered through schools, has been given a different spin, too—it draws on a far broader range of reading materials, with an emphasis on cultural and gender diversity. The adult program, though it now seems like something of a cultural dinosaur, still carries on its original mission, with an estimated 20,000 adults now participating in about 1,800 Great Books groups around the country (the junior program reaches 800,000 children). And some of these adult groups have been meeting for forty years, presumably doing a lot of rereading.

According to Lonnie Plecha, senior editor of the Great Books Foundation, the Foundation revises the reading lists every decade or so. Back in the late 1970s and early 1980s, the focus shifted to short fiction for a while, with authors like Flannery O'Connor and Isak Dinesen welcomed into the ranks. But the current offerings are more or less back to what Adler and Hutchins started with: Plato's *The Apology,* Shakespeare's *Othello,* Hobbes's *Origin of Government,* Maimonides's *On Evil,* Weber's *The Spirit of Capitalism,* Kafka's *The Metamorphosis,* and Gogol's *The Overcoat* are some of the Great Books of today. Plecha acknowledges that the Great Books have come under criticism in recent years for being insufficiently politically correct: "We are aware of the attacks and we are sensitive to them. But it's important to say that we don't feel we are trying to choose a canon of the best books ever written. Ultimately the Great Books movement is about *discussions* of good literature. We don't have a political agenda. We don't claim to stand for Western culture." The entire Great Books program takes five years to complete, with fifteen titles assigned each year. (For information about joining or starting a Great Books group, contact The Great Books Foundation, 35 East Wacker Drive, Suite 2300, Chicago, IL 60601–2298, tel. 800–222–5870.)

Sociologist Elizabeth Long believes that the Great Books movement was the direct forerunner of today's book group explosion, as many people split off from the Great Books regimen to form more relaxed, wide-ranging book groups of their own design. The Great Books list has lost some of its cultural authority, but the impulse to gather in small groups to discuss literature has remained remarkably persistent through the years.

Why have book groups resurged in the past couple of decades? That's open to speculation. Jill Dunbar, of Three Lives & Company bookstore in New York City, notes, "This generation is probably the last real reading generation in America. As they're getting older and couch-potatoing more the idea of a reading group is something that's very welcome to them." Virginia Vallentine, the fiction buyer and book group advisor at Denver's Tattered Cover bookstore, says, "My feeling is that the current movement gained momentum from the generation of people now in their thirties and forties. This was the first generation to grow up with television as their primary stimulus and the first generation in which women took working for granted. These young women were working very hard and didn't really have the chance to read. They wanted companionship, intellectual stimulation. They wanted to go back and repattern themselves and they found they could do this by sitting down and reading a book. The books get the groups going. People get so excited by reading these great books." Long draws similar conclusions from her extensive research of contemporary book groups in and around Houston, Texas: "Society does not provide us with a lot of places or associations to do the things that book groups do. They fill holes left in people's lives. Housewives talk about valuing their groups because of the isolation they feel at home with kids. Professional women talk about being isolated from other women. Engineers and others in the sciences say they have no other place to talk about general questions and ideas. They need a break from technical reading and technical discussions. The talk about ideas is important—but book group members link the ideas with sociability. What people most value about their groups is that they get to talk about moral, political, and esthetic issues that they might not get to otherwise. It's a special kind of socializing. The thoughts about books are enriched by having other people's lives to draw on."

Her study of Houston groups (the only broad-based sociological study we have come across) reveals that 60 percent of those Texas groups are all-female, 30 to 35 percent mixed sex, 5 to 10 percent all-male. Most of the members in Long's sample are college-educated, white professionals, though she has found a good sprinkling of African-American groups. She's noticed a disproportionate number of ex-teachers. All age groups are represented, with the greatest concentration falling in the late twenties to early middle age. Long finds that groups stay together a long time and that once people are admitted they are almost never kicked out (though particularly obnoxious individuals may leave after being "frozen out" by the others). Book groups, she feels, become an important part of people's lives, and people frequently tell her how much they have "been through" with their groups.

Our impression that "everyone" is in a book group these days may be a bit exaggerated, but there is lots of evidence that the movement is cresting. Independent bookstores promote them actively, with book group sign-up sheets and bulletin boards at bookstores. Publishers tie in their authors' promotional tours with visits to book groups, and they develop special book promotions to attract reading groups. *The Wall Street Journal* reported recently that reading groups are now so widespread that publishers credit them with boosting such titles as Kazuo Ishiguro's *The Remains of the Day* and Jill Ker Conway's *The Road from Coorain* onto the best-seller list. The fad has even spread to celebrity circles. A group of high-powered New York intellectuals, including Cynthia Ozick, Harvey Shapiro, and Philip Lopate, met regularly to talk about their verse-by-verse perusal of the Bible. *Vanity Fair* reports that socialities Brooke Astor, Carter and Susan Burden, Anne Bass, and Annette de la Renta are the "nucleus" of a ritzy New York group (their theme for 1994 was memoirs). Barbra Streisand's Hollywood group, which includes superagent Mike Ovitz's wife Judy and Disney head Michael Eisner's wife Jane, has read everything from Jane Austen's *Pride and Prejudice* to Toni Morrison's *Beloved*. Evidently, the rich and famous have been at this for some time. Back in the 1950s, Phyllis Cerf Wagner, Babe Paley, Minnie Astor, Kitty Carlisle Hart, and other grande dames met monthly at the St. Regis Hotel to talk books.

Long feels that today's book clubs have lost some of the high-mindedness and cultural voracity of groups in the past, and we agree. "A lot of the women back in nineteenth-century study clubs were very serious about themselves and about acquiring knowledge and culture," Long asserts. "These women felt that reading Shakespeare and Dickens would ennoble them. Literature does not mean the same thing now. It's no longer so inspirational."

The cultural insecurity that drove a lot of people to join Great Books groups has also waned. Nowadays we tend to have more confidence in our intellectual abilities and in the validity of our opinions. We don't need to be told "how to read a book" (the title of a best-selling book by Great Books movement organizer Mortimer J. Adler). We don't join groups to become conversant with the great minds of the past. We join because we love books and love to talk about books, or because we want a push to read more or read more widely, or because we want to meet fellow book lovers. For many of us, just as for many of our female forerunners back in the nineteenth century, our book groups represent our sole escape from the pressures of home, family, children (and work, which wasn't as true for women a century ago).

We cherish our book groups because here and only here can we kick off our shoes, let our hair down, and say exactly what we feel about subjects we really care about.

Will people in future generations look back at us and say, "Wasn't it *weird* how many people back in the 1980s and 1990s got together in the evenings to talk about Jane Smiley and Barbara Kingsolver and Kazuo Ishiguro and Margaret Atwood? Didn't they have anything better to do with their time?" Maybe. Probably. But who cares? This is our cultural moment. Let's make the most of it.

# 2

# A Group of One's Own

"I was really gung ho about a book club, because I'd been looking for *something*," Rebecca recalls. "Michael had several single-sex activities, and I didn't have anything. We would get into these arguments because he was out several nights a week with his activities, and I'd say, 'I never get to do anything like that,' and he'd say, 'Well, you can. I'll baby-sit.' But there wasn't anything. What the hell was I going to do? Go wrap bandages somewhere, you know?" she laughs wryly. "Candy striping? But this was one thing that really interested me, so when my friend called, I jumped on it."

Rebecca's book club, made up of ten professional women in their late thirties and early forties, had its first meeting over Edith Wharton's *The House of Mirth,* and Rebecca was hooked. But although the group read a string of good books its first year, they began to disagree over what books to read and had some lackluster discussions. Rebecca joined another newly starting book club (also all women), just in case her first one died. Both groups survived, however, and now she has two nights a month devoted to book clubs—and two books a month to plow through.

Meanwhile, Michael, watching her rip through the reading group books month after month, got interested. He would often read the same book that month, vicariously enjoying the group through her. After a year or so, Michael decided he'd like to join a book club too. Rebecca wasn't interested in finding a coed group for them to join together—"This is the only thing I have that's just mine," she declares. Eventually, his college alumni club started a coed reading group, and he joined.

Brad and Wendy's case is somewhat similar. Soon after they started living together, he was asked to join an existing coed book club by a friend who knew that Brad was an omnivorous reader. Wendy began to want to join a group too, to encourage herself to read more. "The way I was working, I never read anymore—and I was living with Brad who'd read everything that ever was written," she says. So when a friend asked her to join an existing group of women, she was thrilled.

A couple of years later (Wendy and Brad got married in the interim), Brad's group split into two, and for a while he went not only to the original group's meetings but to the splinter group's meetings too. Wendy occasionally attends Brad's groups (both factions) as well as her own, and she can clearly see the differences in their styles. Brad's groups, for instance, spend most of their time on book discussion, while her group is more social—and that's precisely what she loves about it.

Social or analytical. Classic or contemporary. Very serious or very frivolous. Style makes all the difference in a reading group. Whether you are about to start your own book club, hoping to join an existing group, or trying to sustain the group you're in currently, it's a good idea to know what you're getting into. After talking to members of reading groups all over the country, one thing has struck us: These are really quite magical institutions. Considering their informal, voluntary nature, it's a wonder how they manage to hang together year after year. But they do, and each one develops its own definite personality, a personality that's somehow greater than the sum of all the members.

The two main elements of a book club are the books you read and the people you read them with. The books you read change from month to month; over the years members may drop out or move away and new recruits will join. But underneath it all, the reading group is guided by some coherent philosophy: This is who we are and this is what we read. And defining that philosophy is what this chapter is all about.

## Look at Your Goals

Why do you want to be part of a reading group? At first, the answer may seem obvious: you want to get together with other people to discuss books. But within that simple ambition are several different shades of interest, and the book club will live or die by how well its members share the same goals.

Which of the following profiles best describes your reason for joining a book club?

- *I'm not reading enough books anymore.* Many people we've talked to are busy professionals or mothers of young children, whose time is consumed by pressing daily demands. The obligation to read one book a month for a book club enforces a kind of discipline on them, and the meeting date gives them a "deadline" by which to read it. If you're this sort of reader, however, be careful not to get into a group that insists on everyone finishing the book and doing extra research—you may not always be able to fulfill those expectations.

- *I'm not reading the right kinds of books anymore.* Within a reading group, various members will suggest interesting new books that you may not have heard of, or will challenge you to read some difficult books that you would have avoided otherwise. If that's what you want a group for, be willing to go along with other people's book choices, even if it's something you wouldn't automatically like. Beware, though, of getting into a group where people don't want to stretch themselves or where there's a certain sameness to their choices. If you're starting a new group, ask prospective members what they've read lately on their own; if you're joining an existing group, ask for a list of what the group has read in the past.

- *I feel like I don't really understand or appreciate the books I do read.* If you approach a reading group as a sort of informal literature course, make sure it delivers the goods. Knowing that you're going to be discussing a book forces you to read it more attentively, and as one woman said of her group, "After our discussion, I've seen more things in the book than I would ever have seen on my own—it made me like books that I didn't like, going into the meeting." But you may want something more: a teacher. Many groups make use of "presenters"—either an ongoing leader/teacher, or a member of the group assigned on a rotating basis to take charge of one month's discussion (see box "Teacher, Teacher" on page 36). Presenters usually open the meeting with a brief lecture on research they have done beforehand; they may also function as discussion leaders, keeping the conversation moving and on track.

- *I want to make some new friends outside of my career or my family.* Regular monthly meetings allow members to get to know each other well, without being defined by their place in the office hierarchy, or without always being "Brian's mommy." If this is what you're looking for, make sure that your sources of members are varied. We talked to one group, for example, that four lawyers in the same firm founded. They made sure that every new member that was added was not a lawyer. Another group was formed by a nurse and two doctors who work at the same hospital, but the other people they invited to join were explicitly not medical people. And make sure, too, that the group you join spends a certain amount of each evening simply socializing—you may not be able to expand on book club friendships if all you know about each other is what you say about the books.

● *I want to get out of the house on my own once in a while.*   It's probably no surprise that the biggest single demographic group among book club joiners is mothers of young children. Another big segment is made up of married women who want an activity away from their spouses: many members of all-women clubs we talked to said firmly that their husbands were never invited to meetings and special outings, and would never be. If your interest in a book club is primarily social, though, a club with demanding book choices and intensive discussions may be too much work for you.

● *I want to catch up on all the classics I didn't read in college.*   Disagreements over which books to read can be very divisive, so make sure from the outset that everybody in the group is in accord on this issue. Consider prospective members in terms of their college majors and their present-day jobs. Someone who was an English major in college may be willing to reread some of the classics, but he or she may not have the same enthusiasm as a physician who, with med school behind her, now has time to find out why people are always talking about *Pride and Prejudice* and *Great Expectations.* And a writer or an editor will have a very different reason for reading contemporary fiction than a computer engineer would.

- *I want to discuss literature as a person, not as a student.* Whether you're reading the classics or contemporary fiction, in a reading group you can feel free to criticize a book, not just in terms of the writer's skill and style but in terms of whether it's true to life or worth writing about. "A lot of people read these things about deconstructionism and so forth, and they think analysis of writing has to be very technical," one book club member said to us. "But after all, if you read books from, say, the mid-nineteenth century through the late 1970s, the writers just expected you to relate to it as a human being. In my book club, people are not pedantic—the feeling is, 'If you don't agree with me, fine'—they're just going to give you *their* viewpoint of the book." For this kind of discussion, you'll need self-confident, well-read people who take books seriously. (There's nothing more frustrating to a book lover than someone who simply yawns, "I couldn't get into it" and didn't read beyond page 45.) It helps if the people are a little older, a little further away from their college experience.

- *I miss the kinds of intellectual discussions I used to have in college.* Some groups enjoy arguing more than others do, and certain members may play devil's advocate in order to provoke discussion. Other groups are more reverential toward the "classics" or more careful not to hurt the feelings of those who did like a certain book. To make sure the quality of book talk is just what you want, sit through a trial discussion before you commit to meeting regularly. And once you're in a group, do everything you can to make sure that the books chosen are ones that will inspire good discussion.

## Book Clubs with a View

Besides the goals listed above, some groups may form with a specific purpose—either the membership is narrowly defined (a lesbian/gay group, or a group of Jewish couples, or a group of schoolteachers) or the members have agreed to read only a certain kind of book (books by women writers or by African-American writers, for instance).

Deliberately restricting membership to a certain kind of person works fairly well—after all, most groups have their own self-selecting membership criteria of one kind or another, whether they admit them or not. The virtue of organizing such a book club is to create a sort of group comfort, which will help guide the discussion into certain channels and make it simpler to choose which books to read.

Susan, who's in a lesbian/feminist group in Denver, notes that her group works because there are still differences of opinion among its members: "Our founder intentionally chose people with a variety of interests. Our politics are similar but we have very different personal styles, from 'way lipstick' to 'totally butch.' We bring in strong opinions—this enhances the discussions. People challenge each other, but it isn't abrasive. There's also a lot of humor. Everyone is willing to laugh at themselves and each other."

The danger sometimes comes in people being *too* similar, which limits the group's response to books. One woman described to us her group of upper-middle-class women in "tartan skirts and turtlenecks" sitting around trying to get a handle on *Waiting to Exhale,* a lively novel by Terry McMillan, a contemporary black woman. "It was awkward for twelve white women to talk about relations between black women and men," she admits. "It felt unreal."

Reading along one theme can also be invigorating: spotting parallels and patterns among the various books you've read brings a nice depth and richness to book discussions. But theme reading can limit the longevity of the group. There may not be enough really interesting books on that topic to keep you going for several years, for one thing. And your discussions may begin to sound like a broken record, as we hear happened for one group that intended to read only feminist classics.

Or the theme may have a built-in limit to it—for instance, if your goal is to read the complete works of Shakespeare or of Trollope, or to do a minute book-by-book study of the Bible, or to have a detailed reading of *Finnegans Wake,* just to mention a few groups we've heard of people starting.

One alternative is to choose a theme for a year—novels about families, for example, or Latin American fiction. This approach works particularly well for groups that want to systematically fill in the gaps in their literary education. It helps if you choose the entire year's book list at the outset, just to make sure you have some idea of where you're going (substitutions can always be made later if you change your minds). We even heard of a group that spent a year reading books with "House" in the title. It sounds silly and arbitrary, but when you consider the books they read—*Bleak House* by Charles Dickens, *The House of Mirth* by Edith Wharton, *The House of the Spirits* by Isabel Allende, *The House of the Seven Gables* by Nathaniel Hawthorne, *The House in Paris* by Elizabeth Bowen, and *The Small House at Allington* by Anthony Trollope—it wasn't such a bad idea.

## Cast of Characters

Before you start inviting individual members, you'll need some definition of what kinds of people you want your group to include. Perhaps the most important variable is gender. By far the largest number of reading groups are all-women, which won't surprise you if you've read Chapter 1.

The difference between an all-women's group and a

mixed-gender group is considerable. People who've been in both kinds point out that in coed groups, discussions all too often focus on male-female terms—how a woman reacts to something versus how a man does. Men and women make markedly different book choices too. As one Denver woman says of the mixed-gender group she used to belong to, "Men wanted books on stars and science books. I ended up dropping out." Another woman we spoke with dropped out of a mixed-sex group, complaining that none of the men knew much about current fiction—she says it cramped her style to have to explain over and over the difference between Alice Munro and Alice Walker. Now she's in an all-women group and she finds conversation flows a lot more freely because they all share the same frame of reference. Some women tell us that they can just relax more around other women: even when they're all arguing aggressively, the group has a nice cozy feeling that they prize. But sharing insights with someone who has a different frame of reference can be very stimulating. And, let's face it, coed groups often have an undercurrent of sexual attraction running between members, which adds a fascinating dimension (this may be why women's groups with lesbian members are so lively).

So what happens to the mix when the men and women in the group are all married to each other? Something good, it seems, because a lot of all-couples groups out there are going strong. The couples we talked to like their book clubs because it gives them a worthwhile social occasion together at least a month. And it gives them a shared intellectual interest, reviving those old bonds that drew them to each other in the first place. As one man said, "My wife and I rarely discuss intellectual topics for sustained periods—we rarely discuss books. She's a big reader. Really, she twisted my arm to join. But I thought it would be a good opportunity to talk about intellectual subjects with a group of intelligent people."

All the people we talked to pointed out that the couples in their groups have to have very strong marriages. Otherwise, with their spouses always present, they wouldn't be able to speak freely and choose to disagree—although one man noted that in each couple, there's generally one partner who speaks up a good deal more than the other. Books about adultery or troubled marriages—such as *Middlemarch, Madame Bovary, Anna Karenina,* or just about anything by John Updike—can be really painful for some married couples to read and discuss.

All-male groups are another deal altogether, and a much rarer species. We've heard of one, in Seattle, which was founded because the men's wives had belonged to a book group for some years. One of its members, Larry, told us, "We felt the need for regular serious reading and to express our feelings about books we read. We had no real philosophy. The idea was, 'Let's get together and choose books we like.' " The men's group is now defunct. Another men's group got together when the men's movement was cresting a few years back, but quickly splintered when they discovered how few books on this topic there really were. The guys interested in reading kept on with the book club, while the others did male bonding and read the occasional short treatise on men's issues.

Another important variable is age. In general, the book clubs we interviewed consist of people who are all the same age, spanning no more than a decade between the oldest members and the youngest ones. The founding members basically invited their friends, who were their own age, and those friends asked along other friends—also their own age—and the whole thing ended up fairly homogenous.

But we did talk to a couple of groups that had wider ranges of ages, generally because they were formed as an offshoot of some other organization. In some of those groups, the range of ages ran all the way from late twenties to early seventies. And all of these book club members cited this mix of ages as a factor in the group's success. "People of different ages bring different experiences and perspectives to the books they read, and that keeps everybody on their toes," one woman said. "Often, when I'm on my way to a meeting, the one person whose reaction to the book I'm most curious about is Alice, our oldest member."

Even with the groups that are generally close in age, we noticed that people made a point of telling us about the one member who was the oldest, or the youngest, and what an invaluable addition she or he is to the group. For example, Denise points out that in her group of Washington-area writers, the oldest member is a veteran reporter who covered the Vietnam War and has traveled all over the globe; his perspective on certain books, especially international fiction, really enlightens the other members. And Ann, whose group of Florida women are generally over sixty years old, says of the one member who's around fifty, "Without Ruth Ann, I'd never have known who Beavis and Butt-head are."

Sociologist Elizabeth Long remarks, "I've noticed that it helps in the longevity of a group if the members are quite a bit alike but not too much. The large-scale demographics should be similar, but there should be enough individual variations so that you don't just get the same viewpoint. There's a balancing act between similarity and difference that keeps the groups healthy."

## How Big a Group?

How many members should you round up before you begin meeting? Our old group started with just four people, gathered around the kitchen table in Debby and Dan's apartment. One new person was invited to the next meeting, and another a couple of months after that. At our largest, we had only nine members.

Other groups we've talked to began with a bang—as many as twenty people came to their first meeting. A few eventually dropped by the wayside, though, leaving a manageable-sized core to continue meeting.

There is no hard-and-fast rule for how many people you need to start a group, or to keep it going happily. The quality and commitment of members matter more, really, than the quantity. In forming a book club, it's important to make sure that you've got enough people that a few absentees or a couple of nonfinishers won't hamper discussion. You can't expect that every member will be able to make it to every meeting—no matter how carefully you consider your next meeting date, by the time it rolls around someone is likely to be unable to attend, for whatever perfectly good reason. But you can have a good meeting with only four people, *if* all four of them have read the book and have strong opinions about it. In fact, a couple of the most exciting meetings our old group ever held—one on Thomas Mann's *The Magic Mountain* and another on Martin Amis's *London Fields*—had only three people present.

On the other hand, the bigger the group, the harder it is for everyone to feel comfortable speaking up—or to get a chance to speak. Michael's book club, which is run by his college alumni club, sometimes had thirty-five or forty people at a meeting. "You can't have a serious clash of values with a group that large," he says. "When there *is* disagreement, various people start to splinter off into little groups. It's sometimes hard to get a word in on the discussion too. There are three or four people who usually dominate the discussion." Interestingly, this club has a somewhat fluctuating membership, but there's a core group of about ten people who come consistently month after month, have always read the book, and try to join in the discussion. When all is said and done, we imagine, those ten people are the real reading group—the others are just onlookers.

Kristen Kennell, of Elliott Bay Books in Seattle, has encountered groups with as many as twenty-four people, but she says that usually only twelve show up for any given meeting. Twelve is also a magic number for Helen, the presenter who runs Ginny's group in suburban Washington, D.C.: "She feels if you get too many people there, then everybody doesn't get to join in the discussion," Ginny says.

The founders of Ann's book club in Florida set their limit at eight. "They want to keep the group small," Ann says, "because they feel that anything bigger would lead to a classroom situation, and they want an intimate discussion."

With an all-couples group, you may need a slightly larger number, since no-shows usually run in pairs. Stewart's group has eight couples—sixteen individual members—but usually only six couples show up on any given evening, which brings it in at twelve people.

## Recruiting Strategies

Choosing the right individuals to join the group sounds terribly important, but—sadder but wiser—we'd like to advance the radical notion that it doesn't really matter. Reading groups have been known to put up with unsuitable members for years—people who never read the book, who don't contribute to the discussion, who have totally different tastes and ideas from the rest of the group, even those who regularly piss off everybody else. Somehow, like any good family, the group absorbs these conflicts and surmounts them. And, in fact, the conflicts themselves often make the meetings more invigorating.

If you're trying to start a group, of course, the logical place to start is among your friends and acquaintances. Here's the most common scenario: A and B, who've been pals since college, decide to form a book club. A asks C, a friend from her office, to join. B asks his old prep school friend D. D happens to have a neighbor, E, whose bookshelves always look interesting. E's son goes to preschool with F's daughter. And at the last minute C brings along G, who used to date the best friend of C's ex-husband. And once they all get in a room together, A discovers that she met G at her cousin's wedding. . . .

Every group we talked to could give us a minute dissection of who was friends with whom and how each member got into the group—it's part of every group's unique thumbprint. People seem to be acutely conscious of which members were originally close friends, and which were sort of outsiders. Those distinctions remain indelibly printed on every member's consciousness, even though the new people are quickly absorbed into the group and made to feel a part of it.

Of course, you wouldn't ask just *any* friend to join. At some point in some conversation, you must have gathered that that friend liked to read and would have interesting things to say. And when people accept the invitation to join, they should be made to realize that it is a sizeable commitment. A reading group in Florida told us that its founders, Nancy and Polly, announced to prospective members in no uncertain terms that you had to be a good reader to join and that you ought to finish the book every meeting ("A couple of people maybe fudge a little, but most do finish it," a member testifies). The women they spoke to were casual acquaintances, all of whom lived in the same sprawling resort community. They all used to see one another around the golf course, pool, and tennis courts, but the reading group now has given them a special bond, and they tend to make golf dates with each other more often.

In fact, it may be fatal to form a book club of really close friends. One New York City group is made up of old dear friends who wanted to meet regularly once a month and sort of tacked on the book discussion. Its members sounded like just the kind of people for a stimulating reading circle: a college English professor, a book editor, a children's librarian, and a bookstore manager. "But we're all really lazy," Felice, the bookstore manager, sighs in exasperation. "We do the reading and all, but nobody does any background research, and the whole thing just sort of degenerates into gossip—we end up not having discussed the book at all. I think you can't do it with friends."

And you don't really need to do it with friends. As Elliott Bay Books's Kristin Kennell points out, it's not all that hard to assemble a bunch of people for a group. "People don't realize how many people are out there—it's really anyone who reads," she urges. "Think about your church, kids' play group, health club, folks at the office. . . . Get three or four people and have all of them talk it up. Have them say, 'Oh, I'm going to my book club . . .' You'll be amazed at how soon you'll find new members."

Vivien Jennings, president of Rainy Days Books in Fairway, Kansas (outside Kansas City), helped organize a book group consisting of mothers and daughters and daughters-in-law. A core of three friends hatched the idea and they networked their way into a group of about twenty women, whose ages range from the mid-twenties to mid-seventies. Now other mother-and-daughter groups have cropped up in the Kansas City area—imitation is surely the sincerest flattery.

We've also talked to some quite successful groups that do no screening whatsoever of their members. Denise started her reading group simply by putting an ad in the Washington Independent Writer's Group newsletter. The ad still runs in every issue, announcing the next meeting's time, place, and subject book. Anyone who wants to drop in can. As a result, there's a fringe of less-committed people who turn up for a couple months at a time and then lose interest. But there's a core group of regulars who really keep the group going, and they're all people who didn't even know each other before the first meeting. "These are people I probably wouldn't have picked as my friends," Denise says, "but it's nice to spend time with people you don't work with. People say very bright things sometimes, and you don't often hear people say bright things at work. . . . It's not too intimate, but it's not superficial either. It allows me to reveal that part of me that I like, the part that loves books, that I don't get to reveal as often."

Michael's Cornell Club book group works the same way, with a continual ad in the club newsletter. "The curious thing about the group is that a lot of people know each other by face and by what you bring to the meeting—they don't really know each other personally," Michael muses. "But people *know* one another, and they know what your bias is going to be, at least for those who participate in the discussion. For instance, for one of the books we were reading, one of the women turned to me and said, 'Now what do *you* think about this issue'—she knew that I had a particular line on that subject from things I'd said about at another meeting."

One of us started a book group out of the local Mount Holyoke Club with a one-time ad in the newsletter; a few of the people who showed up at the first meeting fell by the wayside, but six of the original women are still in the group. We didn't run the ad again because we already had enough readers to get going, and we wanted a consistent membership. Over the next year, three more committed readers came along, a couple of whom aren't even Mount Holyoke alumnae. None of these women really knew each other before they joined this book club, but there's a palpable sense now of their being a reading community.

How else can you meet the right "strangers" to join your book club? Independent bookstores are a wonderful source (they're a wonderful resource for reading groups in general). Elliott Bay Books in Seattle, the Tattered Cover in Denver, Prairie Lights in Iowa City, Rainy Day Books in Fairway, Kansas, the Book Passage in Corte Madera, California, Dutton's Brentwood Books in Los Angeles, Sam Weller's Zion Bookstore in Salt Lake City, and Baxter Books in Minneapolis are among the bookstores where staff members can help reading groups get organized, down to helping them develop a list of books to read. Elliott Bay Books has a bulletin board where like-minded readers can find one another to form their own reading groups; so does Shakespeare & Company in New York City and Powell's Bookstore in Portland, Oregon. If your local bookstore doesn't provide this service, see if they will institute it—it wouldn't take much effort on their part, and it could be great for their business.

Other community service bulletin boards—at colleges, YMCAs, churches and synagogues, public libraries—may help other readers find each other to start book clubs. Also consider which local newsletters or small newspapers may be suitable places to put in an ad calling for interested readers. Think about local chapters of national organizations, such as the American Association of University Women, which organized several book groups we've heard about. Or contact your state humanities foundations—several of them organize reading groups in conjunction with the National Book Foundation, with an annual reading list on one theme, local scholars leading discussion circles, and readings by National Book Award winners. In fact, any time a novelist or poet is giving a reading in your community, seize the opportunity to hook up with other book lovers there.

Once initial contact has been made with possible members, you'll need to interview one another to make sure your reading goals are compatible. But don't be too picky—give one another a chance. After a few meetings, people who aren't "right" for the group usually fade out of the picture, almost by magic. But what remains is a core of people determined to stick together and make the group work.

Your other option may be to hook up with a group that's already going. Several people we interviewed had joined their groups a few years after they were founded, and they now feel very much a part of the club. When members move or drop out for various reasons, a group generally acknowledges that it needs new people in order to survive, and makes an effort to bring in new blood. Beware, however, of a group whose membership is a revolving door—chances are that people are dropping out because there's something wrong with the group.

If you know people who are in reading groups already,

hint strongly that you'd love to be invited if they ever have an opening. You may have to wait a year or two (be sure you keep reminding your friend of your interest!), but be patient. Or stick up a notice on bulletin boards at local bookstores, colleges, and community centers—if a group is looking for new blood, they'll be pleased to find out about you.

When you find an existing group that's interested in you, ask to sit in on one group meeting—preferably two—before committing yourself to joining. That way you can sample the level of discussion, the ratio of social conversation to book discussion, etc. But be tactful about this "audition"—people already in the group may be offended if a prospective member sounds too choosy. They probably feel that they are conferring an honor just by inviting you to join.

## What Do You Want to Read?

Different groups have different procedures for choosing which books they read—in Chapter 3 we'll discuss these various procedures. But from the outset, there should be a consensus about what kinds of books will be read. You can't expect everyone in the group to like exactly the same kinds of books—that would really make discussions dull—but there should be some agreement about the kinds of books you'll try.

The majority of book groups read novels and nothing else. Our guess is that this is because fiction is more emotionally absorbing than nonfiction—with stories you can lose yourself in, characters you can relate to, situations that move you to tears or to laughter. Fiction elicits strong feelings, and strong feelings in turn fuel good discussion. People also tend to consider fiction to be more "fun" reading, and it's certainly far removed from the informational reading most of us are forced to do in our daily work. Or maybe it's because most people are still harking back to college, hoping to experience those literature classes they never got around to taking.

Within the realm of fiction, though, book clubs are all over the place. One group's reading list is full of best-sellers; another is full of "new fiction" and self-consciously artistic contemporary writing. Current novels by and largely about women are favorites in many, many groups. One group concentrates on American literature, another on British novels.

### Teacher, Teacher

If people want the reading group experience to be quasi-academic, they may consider having a presenter. We'll discuss how this works at greater length in Chapter 4, but if you want your group to have a paid professional as a leader, you'll have to decide that at the outset. Every prospective member of the group should be aware that this is part of the deal, and should be willing to pay his or her own share.

Most groups with paid presenters are started by some kind of institution, such as a YMCA, an alumni group, or a public library. That was the case with Ginny's group in Washington, D.C.; but after one semester as an organized class, it had enough momentum to continue privately, and it's been going strong for sixteen years now.

If a private group wants to hire its own presenter, that person should be in place before the group can really get started. Sources for finding presenters include local colleges, good independent bookstores, and a vigorous word-of-mouth campaign ("does anybody know of anybody who might be willing to . . ."). We

One group may read lots of international fiction, while another group has a rule of thumb: "Nothing in translation." Most groups we talked to claimed to read a mix of modern novels and classics, but for some people the classics end of that mix comes down to one nineteenth-century novel a year, while others enjoy a steady diet of Thomas Hardy, Henry James, and Jane Austen, with the occasional Shakespeare play thrown in.

When you're first organizing a group, try to define the

---

have heard of a couple of people in large cities who lead four or five groups professionally—working as academics without portfolio, they've found this way to use their Ph.D.s in English literature without having to join a college faculty.

When you find a presenter, you'll need to work out a fair fee for this work and then split the fee among all prospective members. If the group is very large, you may be able to get by with charging members on a meeting-by-meeting basis, but most groups agree on an annual fee, almost like tuition for a class. That signals an ongoing commitment on the part of both the presenter and the members, which is important.

Another option is having members of the group rotate as presenters, or at least as moderators responsible for keeping the discussion moving along. But be sure that all prospective members agree from the outset that they are happy to do this. Some people inevitably will be better presenters than others, but at least if everyone *says* from the beginning that they're willing to do their turn, they're more likely to make the effort.

kinds of books you're hoping to read, giving specific titles as examples. In Denise's book club, "There were a couple of members early on who wanted to read things like *Jurassic Park* and best-sellers like that," she recalls. "But the rest of us didn't want to go in that direction, so those people kind of faded out." The final issue that split Brad's group in two was a feeling that their reading was getting too "lightweight."

"Over the course of the three years I've found that the really satisfying choices were classics," Rebecca says. "A few of the more modern books have been worthwhile, but by and large, the disasters have been the Mona Simpsons and so forth. A lot of times these modern books were picked just because of word-of-mouth—but you don't get word-of-mouth on classics, people don't go around saying, 'Oh, I've heard William Dean Howells is good,' you know? You've got to find out about them and read them yourself."

If you plan to read lots of classics, it's a good idea to have the tools to do them right. An ex-English major or two can be tremendously helpful in steering the group through issues of narrative techniques in Henry James, tragic structure in Thomas Hardy, or metaphor and symbol in Shakespeare. Discussion will also be more focused if someone is willing to do background research on each book. A couple of people we talked to found themselves in the position of being the "expert" every time their group read classics—neither of them minded playing this role, but they felt the group wouldn't have been able to appreciate the book without them.

We also suggest that you declare from the outset that novels will not be the only books you'll read. "People are often reluctant to do nonfiction," one bookstore manager told us. "They think it will be a geology text. But actually lots of groups love it when they finally take the plunge." Nonfiction works best if the book is controversial or has some interesting method of presentation. Nature essays and travel writing are long on description, so they're easier to read than social criticism or history, where much of the discussion will center on content. Biographies are a good nonfiction choice, perhaps because the story of a person's life is much like a novel. Biographies of writers are especially fun, read in conjunction with the writer's books.

Self-help and pop psychology books do crop up on reading groups' lists from time to time, but the members generally don't feel they make for good discussion. We have heard of a book club that reads only self-help books, but it sounds as if it functions as a support group or amateur therapy group as much as a book club, and apparently they've broken up and gotten back together again a couple of times.

Of course, a group's ideas of what books to read change with time. Our old reading group originally was formed to read only twentieth-century American novels, but that rule was broken at the very first meeting, when we read Samuel Beckett's novel *Molloy,* written by an Irishman living in France. We went on to read poetry, plays, essays, travel writing, science books, a spy novel, and a murder mystery; we read books from Europe, Asia, and South America, as well as the United States; and we read things that had been written as long ago as the fifteenth century (we even talked about reading the *Iliad* and the *Odyssey* but never got around to it). In short, we read what we wanted to, once we had a bead on everybody's level of appreciation.

"It's my impression that as groups mature, their book choices get more focused," says Michael, whose group is still only eight months old. "After they've been in existence about three or four years, perhaps they start to develop a theme." Well, maybe. One thing is true: no matter how long a group has been around, choosing the specific books to read, month after month, is probably the most absorbing and contentious task a reading group faces . . . but more of that in the next chapter.

# 3

# Standard Operating Procedures

There are two ways to go with a new reading group's first meeting: You can make it an organizational meeting, where you plan and discuss how your group is going to operate, or you can just take the plunge and start off by discussing a book you've all agreed on in advance.

A lively book discussion could really inspire everybody to keep coming—or else it could backfire and scare them all off. Denise recalls, "We read *Mating* for our first meeting. I can't even remember the author—I must be blocking it. God, that was an awful book. I'm surprised the group kept on meeting after that." (The author, by the way, is Norman Rush, and lots of other groups loved this book choice—go figure.)

"The first time you go is critical," says Chris, whose Seattle-area group is still in its first year. "You can't really quit after that without feeling that you are somehow making a statement. My wife wanted to quit after the first meeting—people were too opinionated, it was too ego-dominated." But they persevered, and meetings have gotten better since then.

We tend to advise starting off with a planning meeting. For one thing, it helps to have the members agree on all the ground rules at the beginning, so that you're not struggling with a lot of organizational issues for the first year. In this chapter, we'll help you see the various ways of setting up your book club so that it has a good chance of surviving.

Of course, even at a planning meeting, you'll all want a chance to assess everyone's personality and commitment to the project. Unless everyone knows each other very well, it's sort of like a collective first date, with various people trading information about themselves and feeling their way toward a relationship. As each new member introduces himself or herself, you could ask that they talk about the last couple of books they enjoyed reading—that should get everyone going in the right vein.

And planning for the future will inevitably generate more book discussion. "At our first meeting, our organizational meeting, we had this book blitz," Rebecca says of her New York City group. "We came up with a big long list of everything we'd ever considered reading—there were twenty-five to thirty books on it. Then we picked our first three books to read, and we were off."

# Where

The vast majority of book clubs meet at the homes of members, but there are some exceptions. Some groups meet at public places, often because the group was originally organized by that institution—a library, a college alumni club, a bookstore, or a school. We've come across a couple of groups that meet regularly at restaurants, which may be expensive but saves individual members the hassle of hosting at their homes.

The at-home groups generally rotate through the homes or apartments of the various members. This rotation is flexible, based on who's going to be in town and available and without house guests, etc. In our experience, most people are eager to host a meeting—it's never hard to find a volunteer, even for groups in which feeding the whole gang is part of the deal.

As a rule, all the members in a group live close enough to make this feasible. Some people's homes may be more convenient than others—as, for instance, with Judy's book club in Cambridge, Massachusetts, where three of the members work at the same hospital. Since Judy lives within walking distance of the hospital, she ends up hosting the group more often than the others do. The one member who lives in a distant suburb is more likely to host the group in the summer, when they can sit outside around his pool.

Two women at the organizational meeting for one new New York City book club expressed some hesitation about hosting—one because her apartment is so small, the other because she lives way out in the borough of Queens. As it turned out, the woman with the small apartment has hosted the meetings quite successfully. (One summer evening, they met on the roof of her apartment building, which was fun.) But the woman who lives out in Queens soon dropped out of the group—it was hard enough for her to get home late at night after meetings, let alone for the other members to get back into Manhattan from her home.

But geographical distance shouldn't be so daunting. After our old reading group had been running strong for a few years, one of us moved out to the suburbs, but the whole group happily took the commuter train out for those occasional evenings. Another person who joined the group later didn't even live anywhere near Manhattan—his home was in northwestern Connecticut. On the evenings when it was his turn to host, he'd "borrow" another member's apartment, bringing in all the food and drink and tending to the hosting duties himself.

This seems to be the usual strategy when a member lives too far away to host. It generally works pretty well—at least until the "out-of-town" members start to outnumber the "in-towners," as happened with Rebecca's group. Their immediate solution was to scrap the idea of serving dinner and switch to brown-bag refreshments, to make hosting a simpler proposition, but it remains to be seen whether all of the suburban members will keep up their commitment to the group.

Conrad is in an all-couples group in which most members live out in scattered suburbs around New York City. Since everybody hosts in their turn, a lot of driving is involved to assemble all the members. This works fine for them, partly because they meet on a Friday night—at eight P.M., so they aren't caught in rush hour traffic. Since they don't have to get up for work the next morning, they don't mind so much if traveling distance makes it a long night.

# When

No matter how dedicated your members are, over the years each of them is going to miss a meeting or two—some more than others. To minimize this, it's very important to set up a scheduling policy that works for everybody.

Many groups we contacted have fixed a precise and unchanging day for their meetings—the third Wednesday of every month, for instance. We're great believers in picking one night of the week that's generally good for everybody, and sticking to it through hell and high water. It helps members to organize their lives, so that they can always make the meetings—if they know, for instance, that reading group is always on a Tuesday, they're not so likely to get a Tuesday night series of concert tickets or sign up for a Tuesday night Spanish class.

Once the group has been going for a while, you can occasionally jockey the dates around, but don't push it too far. Judy's group in Cambridge, Massachusetts, met regularly every first Monday of the month. "Then we started switching it around for various reasons, because somebody had a class or other plans or something—and then things started to fall apart," she says. The lack of consistent meeting dates was probably a symptom of other problems, not a cause, but the group stopped meeting for a whole year, and only recently has gotten back together.

Beyond that caveat, your choice of an evening to meet on depends on the members' schedules. We know of a couple of groups—all-women groups, as it happens—who meet one morning a month. This schedule, however, automatically limits membership to people who don't have office jobs. We've also talked to two groups who meet on weekend nights— Friday or Sunday—but they are all-couples groups, for whom the book club is a special part of their social life.

Most groups, however, meet on weeknights. A couple of people noted that their meetings are on Monday because there tend to be fewer conflicts that day than there are midweek. "Monday's also good because, if you're behind on your reading, you have the weekend to finish the book," one woman admitted with a smile.

Almost every group we've talked to or heard of meets monthly, more or less. There's something magical about the monthly meeting—it gives people enough time to read the book, doesn't take too big a bite out of their spare time, and still meets often enough to assume an important role in their lives. A very few groups manage to meet every other week— and people do get the books read in that short amount of time—but such an ambitious program is probably too daunting for most readers.

Some groups actually end up meeting every five or six weeks, largely because it's too hard to find a mutually convenient date any sooner than that. For instance, one New York group we know schedules its meeting around the dates when one of its members, who moved to western Pennsylvania, can next make it into town.

It seems that all-couples groups have a harder time settling on meeting dates than groups of individuals do. It's hard enough to find a night when both spouses are free, let alone multiplying that by the number of couples in a book club! We can imagine the scenario: twelve middle-aged professional people, date books in hand, furiously conducting complex negotiations about who's likely to be free when.

Several groups have adopted one variation on the monthly theme: they meet only September through May. This academic schedule may appeal to people because the book club feels a bit like school anyway. Members who have younger children may find their schedules altered in summer, with the kids home from school; with families taking summer vacations, or even going away to a summer home, it can get very hard to draw a quorum for reading group meetings. For this reason, other groups at least skip the August meeting, taking the extra month's time to read a longer book for the September meeting. Somehow, the image of spending August on a beach immersed in a thick novel like *War and Peace* or *David Copperfield* is very appealing.

The other time of the year that wreaks havoc with schedules is December, with all its holiday activities and trips. Few groups that we talked to actually skip the December meeting, but they do take the holidays into account when picking the book for the January discussion meeting. Some groups deliberately pick a short book to read over December, because holidays make it harder to read—but others pick a longer book, knowing that there'll be several vacation days from work, giving their members *more* reading time. Still others use the December meeting to exchange gifts (books, of course!), to plan the next year's reading list, or to invite spouses along.

## How Long

It's hard in advance to dictate how long each meeting "should" last. Some meetings will run longer than others, powered by the excitement of that month's book discussion. But every group we talked to fell into its own distinctive pattern, varying surprisingly little from month to month, and members could describe it to us quite clearly.

Evening starting times vary from six-thirty to as late as eight o'clock. A lot of this has to do with whether or not dinner is being served, and what time working people tend to leave their offices. Here are some examples of patterns we've seen:

- Ginny's group meets at ten-thirty in the morning. They stand around in the dining room over coffee and cookies, chatting until eleven A.M. Then their paid presenter, Helen, moves them into another room (a living room, family room, or study, depending on the house), where they sit down for discussion. It usually runs until about one P.M. Helen gives them another book title for the future (generally they work a couple of months ahead, so they already know what next month's book will be). Occasionally some of them will go out to lunch together afterward.

- Michael's group meets at the New York City Cornell Club at six-thirty. A Cornell Club staff person acts as moderator, so the meeting starts fairly promptly, food is served unobtrusively at a side buffet, and the discussion moves along efficiently. At the end, there's a fifteen-minute discussion of which book to read next month. They're usually finished by eight o'clock. Since it's a large group with few social ties, there's less socializing before and after the meeting.

- Denise's group, in Washington, D.C., meets at six-thirty, too, but their meetings usually run about two-and-a-half hours. Since most people come straight from work, snack food is served. There's a lot of gabbing at first, then somebody—usually Denise—gets the discussion going. It usually lasts for an hour or an hour-and-a-half. Then comes the hard part—picking next month's book—which takes at least another half hour.

- Ann's group meets for about two hours, starting at seven P.M., which is considered postdinner in their Florida resort community. They start by talking about the book for a while, but a good part of the meetings is spent on other topics—current events and local cultural buzz.

- David's group, in Indianapolis, meets at seven-thirty on a Sunday night. After about half an hour of socializing, that month's moderator leads off with a short presentation—the author's biography, the history of the book, etc.—and then asks questions, prompting discussion for about an hour. Then some kind of dessert is served, and there's more socializing.

- Brad's group meets from eight to around ten P.M. Their first half hour is like a cocktail party; then they all sit down to dinner and book discussion begins, with a five-minute presentation by that month's volunteer moderator. At the end, they argue over which book to discuss in two months (they already know what book they're reading for this next month).

- Alice's group meets at seven P.M., and as soon as most of the members are there and have a drink in hand, they launch into the book. A casual dinner is served around eight o'clock. At the first few meetings book discussion would break off then, and the women would pitch into an animated free-for-all conversation over dinner. Too often, however, they didn't really feel "done with the book" yet, so they've been making an effort to steer the talk back onto book discussion while they're eating. (Alice describes this as "the club where everybody talks at once," so there are inevitably a lot of lively digressions anyway.) At about nine, the members with young children say they have to leave, and there's a flurry of discussion on picking next month's book and meeting date.

# Next . . .

As you can see from the various scenarios above, choosing what book to read next is often a major part of a book club meeting—sometimes it's even more lively than the book discussion itself. Picking the right book is important, not only because it means the meeting will be spirited, but also because, for many book club members, this is the only book they'll have time to read this month. They want it to be a good one.

Some groups choose books in advance, several titles at a time. Groups may even plan an entire year's list all at once, especially if they're trying to organize their reading along a specific theme every year. The periodic book-selecting session can be a whale of a good evening, and with several titles to choose, people won't feel frustrated by having to turn down one good book in favor of another.

Book group advisor Kristin Kennell advises the pick-ahead strategy, because it gives people plenty of time to read the books and prevents recurrent wrangling over book choice at the last minute. Vivien Jennings of Rainy Day Books discourages groups from getting themselves locked in *too* far ahead, though: "You may not feel like reading too many heavy books in a row, or some hot new paperback may appear and you'll be frustrated because you're already booked up for the year," she points out. "Two or three months ahead is the best."

Most groups we talked to pick their books on a month-by-month basis, or at the most pick books two months ahead. The two-months-ahead plan gives members sufficient time to get hold of a copy and read it, but it means they still have a book-picking session at the end of every meeting. We really enjoyed this part of our meetings, but several people we talked to said they *hated* it. Find a routine that works for your group.

Of course, different book clubs have evolved different systems to generate book choices. A few operate by fiat— someone, either a paid presenter or the next month's host or moderator, simply tells them what to read. Considering that book clubs are totally voluntary pursuits, this sort of dictatorial approach has its risks. Helen, the professional leader who runs Ginny's group, chooses a book list for them, but she is careful to give the members some input, and after so many years together they've developed a lot of mutual trust. In David's group, each month's moderator gets to dictate his or her book choice, and it's final—no discussion. But that member is expected to have read the book before proposing it, to make sure it is suitable. "There have been some books that nobody finished," he admits. "I picked *East is East,* by T. Coraghessan Boyle, which I loved, but to my surprise no one else liked it. If you pick a difficult book, you've got to expect that some people won't have read it. . . . One woman picked *Clan of the Cave Bear,* and we were pretty merciless—she paid a dear price for picking that book. That's kind of an expectation, if you've got a dog of a book people are just gonna tell you."

At the other end of the spectrum is a totally democratic approach—such as the system Wendy M.'s group of New York City women uses: "The way we choose the books is very organic—we just sort of go on talking until we reach some sort of consensus." Wendy J., who's in a different all-women's group in New York City, echoes this feeling: "That's a hard part for us—we do it last, just before everybody leaves." Sometimes when they're in the midst of choosing, she adds, the host will run over to her shelves and start to read out titles to inspire them. If even one person vetoes a title, they respect that person's feelings and won't choose that book.

The danger with this lovely anarchy is that it may not always work, or it may take too long. Rebecca recalls that in one of the two reading groups she's in, there got to be a good deal of jockeying over who could control what books got picked—a dichotomy, she noted, between people who wanted to read classics and those who wanted to read trendy current fiction. So they instituted a new rule: the hostess of the current meeting has to provide three book suggestions. In the

## Pick Something Besides Novels

We were surprised how few groups we interviewed made an effort to read **short stories**—our old reading group had fabulous discussions about collections of short stories. Certain marvelous writers are at their best in this form: try the Russians, Anton Chekhov and Alexander Pushkin; the Southerners Eudora Welty and Flannery O'Connor; the delightfully acerbic Dorothy Parker; chronicler of the suburbs John Cheever; contemporary Irishman William Trevor; transplanted New Zealander Katherine Mansfield; and minimalist Raymond Carver. With a short story collection, to keep discussion from hopping all over the place, you may want to designate three or four stories as the focus of discussion.

**Poetry** is read even less often by book clubs, which is a shame. Some groups may feel intimidated by poetry, unless there is at least one member who is knowledgeable enough to lead the group on a poetry night. One women's group we talked to had a special poetry night at which each member passed around photocopies of ensuing discussion, other titles can be thrown onto the table, and her final choice may not be one of those original three, but at least one person has nominal control of the process each meeting. This was the system we used in our old reading group, too, and it did have its advantages. For one thing, it meant that somebody always provided some solid book suggestions to get the ball rolling. After meeting for several years, we'd read many of the obvious choices, and that jump start was a useful thing.

her two favorite poems, which they read aloud and discussed. It was a good meeting, and they'd like to do it again sometime. Another group was pleasantly surprised by Robert Browning's dramatic monologues; each member volunteered to take responsibility for studying one poem, and then at the meeting they read them aloud. The five great odes by John Keats could make for a nice focused poetry discussion too. Other poets we'd suggest for readers who haven't done a lot of poetry: Emily Dickinson, Walt Whitman, W. B. Yeats, W. H. Auden, Anne Sexton, Sylvia Plath, Adrienne Rich, Seamus Heaney, and Philip Larkin. Don't try difficult poets— dense poets like T. S. Eliot or Ezra Pound, or exuberantly wordy ones like Dylan Thomas, unless you're sure everyone is ready to grapple with them.

And what about ***plays***? If your group enjoys reading aloud, plays can be a great choice, especially those by playwrights like Shakespeare and G. B. Shaw, full of ideas and marvelous writing. Among more modern playwrights, we'd suggest Tennessee Williams, Eugene O'Neill, Arthur Miller, and Lillian Hellman.

## *Where to Look for Book Choices*

The annotated book lists beginning on page 120 of this book could keep your group reading happily for years. But, like most reading groups, yours will probably want to ferret out your own choices as well. Here are some places to look:

***The New York Times Book Review.*** Beneath the list of hardcover best-sellers, toward the back of the magazine, "And Bear in Mind" mentions a few titles that may not have the mass-market appeal of best-sellers, but are highly recommended by the review's editors. And if your book club has a rule about only reading paperbacks, look for the "New and Noteworthy" column, which highlights notable books that have just been released in paperback.

***ALA Booklist.*** Each year the American Library Association publishes lists of the "best" books of the year in the March 15 issue of its *Booklist* magazine (available at most libraries). Brief summaries of the books are included.

***Major Book Awards.*** Reading groups don't necessarily read a book as soon as it wins a big award (for one thing, many groups wait until it's out in paperback), but lists of prize-winning books usually yield some great suggestions for future group choices. *Pulitzer Prizes* for fiction, poetry, drama, history, biography or autobiography, and general non-fiction are awarded each April. The *Pen Faulkner* fiction prize, awarded to one work of new American fiction, is also announced each April. *National Book Awards*, honoring the year's best fiction, nonfiction, and poetry books, are awarded each November. Both of these two latter awards announce all the finalists in advance; paperback editions will often boast that a book was a National Book Award finalist.

The same is true of Britain's most coveted literary award, the *Booker Prize*, given each year to a novel first published in Britain and written by a U.K. or Commonwealth citizen. Being "short-listed for the Booker" is itself a considerable honor. Britain's other big honor is the *Whitbread Literary Award*, which is given in several categories: novel, first novel, children's novel, poetry, biography, and book of the year. In France, the top literary award is the *Goncourt Prize*. The world's top literary award, the *Nobel Prize for Literature*, is announced each fall, honoring not just one title but the complete work of a writer of international stature.

**Reading Woman.** This newsletter, published out of Minneapolis, features write-ups and excerpts from books that have worked for book groups. Order through Bering Communications, P.O. Box 19116, Minneapolis, MN 55419–9998.

**Ex Libris.** Another book club newsletter, this one runs reading lists and book write-ups. Contact K. Schlosberg, 33 Chandler St., Newton, MA 02158.

**Local booksellers.** Several long-time book club members have developed a relationship with a local bookstore, and they periodically stop in to chat with the owner. Some bookstores have book group advisors who recommend titles and even offer in-store presentations of books tailor-made to various groups. This is a great way to pick up grass-roots recommendations of books that other reading groups have loved.

Your group will probably also want to have certain parameters to guide book choices. Most groups, for example, agree to read only books that are available in paperback, or are easy to find at the public library. "Our one rule is no hardbacks," Brad says, "which we then broke for *A Thousand Acres* because no one wanted to wait until it got into paperback."

Another useful idea is to agree not to read books beyond a certain length. (We heard of a group that didn't want to read books longer than 100 pages, but it didn't last very long!) This will vary from group to group; Brad's club, for instance, sets its limit at a hearty 600 or 700 pages (even so, there are books they've had to reject because they're too long). Ann's book club learned this lesson the hard way, after reading *Pillars of Fire,* a thick historical novel by Ken Follett. Though it was fairly enjoyable, she says, some people thought it was too much to read in a month, and now they're more careful to pick books that are between 250 and 300 pages.

Many groups do manage to work in an occasional long book, however, by saving them for a time when, for one reason or another, there's more reading time between meetings (over a summer hiatus, for example, or during the December holidays). A couple of groups mentioned to us that they had thought about spreading a long book over two meetings, discussing the first half at one meeting, then discussing the rest at a second meeting. But the one group we talked to that had tried this found that most members had run out of things to say by the second meeting.

The flip side also works: If your schedule for some reason gives you only three weeks or so between meetings one month, pick a shorter, lighter book to read.

Other considerations may come into play when choosing what books to read. Denise says that her group, which has both men and women in it, consciously makes an effort to balance between male and female writers. Ann's group, after several months of reading contemporary best-sellers, made a conscious decision to read a classic (they picked *Vanity Fair).*

Other groups have their own crotchets. "No Jane Austen," one member insisted. "Nothing in translation," was the policy one woman laid down for another group. Of course, they've broken that rule three times already this year—always apologizing to her first, of course, in what has become a delicious little in-joke.

## Sources for Titles

Where do suggestions for books to read come from? Everywhere. (See box, "Sources for Book Titles" on pages 52-53.) Individual members may be plugged into the book buzz—Susan's Denver group, for example, has two members who work in bookstores, and they always seem to know what's new and hot. Brad wryly says that one of the reasons he was asked to join his book club, which has lots of investment bankers in it, is that he has read a lot already and keeps in touch with literary currents: "I'm the one who usually brings in the lists of what to read," he notes.

Often, a book is picked because of good published reviews, or because a friend of a friend of one of the members said it was great. But a number of groups told us that, after a few disappointments, they began to require that members propose only books that they had already read. (Sometimes that person rereads it that month, and sometimes not—it depends on the person, the book, and how long ago he or she read it.)

Several people we talked to keep a file folder where they store clippings about books that sound interesting. Since new books are generally reviewed only when they come out in hardcover, you may have to hang on to these for a while until the book is issued in paperback (if it ever is!). We also interviewed a couple of impressively well-organized groups who actually keep a running list of titles that have been suggested at past meetings—the runners-up, so to speak—so that they have a ready-made pool of ideas to begin each book selection session.

Michael's Cornell Club book group went to a logical source: the Cornell faculty, where an English professor recommended that they read something by William Dean Howells, a nineteenth-century American writer they would never have thought of on their own. They duly read Howells's *The Rise of Silas Lapham* and loved it.

Repeating authors you've liked is another good source of titles—Judy's group loved *Palace Walk,* the first volume of a trilogy by Egyptian novelist Naguib Mahfouz, so they went on to read the second book of the trilogy, *Palace of Desire.* They'd probably have read the third book, too, except the English translation hadn't yet come out in paperback. They also loved John Irving's *A Prayer for Owen Meany* so much that a few months later they read his *Ciderhouse Rules* too.

Ginny's group also tends to repeat its favorite authors—they've read six books by Jane Austen, eight by Charles Dickens, eight by Henry James, six by Anthony Trollope, and five by Thomas Hardy. (As you can tell, this group definitely leans toward the classics.) They've even done a few books twice—*The Return of the Native, The Age of Innocence,* and *The Lonely Passion of Judith Hearne* by Brian Moore. This is a long-lived group (it was founded in 1978), and the membership has changed a good deal between the first and second readings, so the subsequent discussions were totally different.

## Guests

In our old reading group, each month's host had the option of inviting a guest. This didn't happen every month, by any means, though there was a year or so when we did it a lot, maybe because we sensed that our discussions needed the spark of new points of view. Perhaps it's no coincidence that when we finally got around to inviting new members, they were people who'd already been visitors—we'd already unofficially "auditioned" them.

A policy regarding guests doesn't have to be set at the very beginning, but it might be useful to raise the possibility early on. Some of the groups we interviewed are quite fluid, with members drifting in and out; a small core of consistent members really keeps it going, and the casual additions are more or less visitors, swelling the numbers and making discussions fresh and lively. Other groups allow members to invite anyone they please to meetings. If the host is serving dinner, though, it's important to insist that the inviting member call the host ahead of time, to add to the head count.

Guests come to book clubs for all sorts of reasons—because they really loved the particular book you're reading, because they're thinking of starting their own book club and want to see how one works, or just because they love book discussions. If you're thinking of inviting a guest, try to make it someone who can hold his or her own in talking about books. Often guests feel timid about jumping into the discussion, sensing that they don't know the other members as well as the members know each other. A particularly argumentative guest can spoil a book discussion, but in the long run that isn't so bad—the rest of you may never see that person again, but you will have gotten some valuable practice in defending your opinions, and the group as a whole will benefit from the controversy.

If your group chooses a book that has some special relevance for someone you know, suggest right off the bat—at the meeting when the book is selected—that you bring him or her along to that meeting. In fact, there may be times when the group might actively look for a guest "expert" on a certain book. The Cornell professor who recommended William Dean Howells to Michael's Cornell Club book group has offered to come down to lead one of their meetings sometime in the future, for instance. If your group is hesitant about trying to read poetry or plays, enlisting a poet or a local theater director for that evening can help you feel your way forward.

Some reading groups have even been able to get the author of the book they're reading to come to their discussion. Keep an eye on local college calendars and bookstores' public reading schedules, and if you see someone good is coming to town, call the writer's publisher and try to coordinate an appearance at your meeting. Publishers, increasingly aware of the importance of book groups, are more and more often willing to arrange such encounters. You probably won't feel free to tear the book apart with the person who wrote it sitting right there, but you'll get wonderful insights on how the book was written—and the writer will get from you the kind of fresh, intelligent feedback that's priceless to any artist.

## Keeping in Touch

Knowing that you'll all see one another at least once a month, the members of your group may not talk to each other at all between meetings—even if they're good friends. When you leave the monthly meeting, you already know where and when you'll meet next time, and you know what book you have to read between now and then. Presumably, you're all set.

But things do come up. What about the people who missed that last meeting—how do they get back in the loop? And what happens if the meeting time has to be changed, or if for some reason the book choice has to be changed?

In our old group, things were very informal. Everybody had one another's phone number, so if there was any change in plans, a series of five phone calls could take care of it— especially after we all got phone machines. The one rule we had was that whoever was slated to be next month's host was responsible for calling anyone who'd missed the last meeting, to fill them in on the pertinent details. People were expected to call the host if they couldn't make the meeting—otherwise, we assumed they'd just show up. For fourteen years, this simple system worked fine for us.

But it isn't always that easy. Calling twelve, or fifteen, or twenty other people is considerably more of a chore than calling five. And if the membership fluctuates, each member may not have all the others' phone numbers.

Two groups we talked to actually send out a flyer between meetings, with the next meeting's date, time, and address at the top. (One of them even plans two months in advance, so you have the succeeding meeting on the flyer, too, like a coming attractions blurb.) These flyers also include a current list of all the members' names and phone numbers, both at work and at home, presumably so that folks can call around and co-ordinate rides with one another. And at the bottom, there's an updated list of the books they've been talking about reading someday. Keeping track of these titles is a super idea, we think. That way, if you happen to be browsing in a bookstore, you can leaf through a copy of a prospective book choice to see what you think of it; or, if you're talking to someone who reads a lot, maybe you can elicit some word-of-mouth opinions on those books *before* the group commits to reading them.

This is a great system—*if* one member of the group is willing to take on this chore, and is organized enough to make sure it gets done (you'll need one person to keep all the relevant stuff on his or her computer, to update it and spit it out month after month).

Short of having a monthly flyer, it is still a good idea to have a formal printed list of members' names, addresses, and phone numbers (home, work, fax, weekend house—anything that might be useful). One member could keep this on a computer and update it periodically, at least once a year, or whenever a new member joins.

It's also immensely useful to keep an updated list of what

books you've read. Perhaps it's no coincidence that the most long-lived and stable groups we talked to could quickly produce a complete list of their books—it says something about how much vigor the group has as an institution. Chances are that there is somebody in your group who likes to keep track of this sort of thing anyway. But if you reach your one-year anniversary and no one has produced such a document, you might enjoy sitting down at a meeting and reconstructing a list of what you've read together. Then get someone to agree to keep the list current from then on.

RSVPs can be a ticklish area. People complained to us that their groups had fallen into the trap of having each month's host call everybody before the meeting, just to get a reliable head count (that's especially essential if you're supposed to be cooking dinner for everybody). Considering that the host already has to clean house, serve refreshments, and possibly act as moderator (not to mention read that month's book), laying this extra burden on him or her seems pretty unfair. We suggest that you insist that all members agree to RSVP to the host. Decide on a clear policy—either they RSVP if they're *not* coming (best for small groups with faithful attendance), or they RSVP if they *are* coming (best for bigger, looser groups).

Perfectly responsible people can miss a couple of meetings in a row, and the danger is that they will drift out of the group if they lose track of where the next meeting is. It's a good idea to set at the beginning a policy on whose responsibility it is to inform absentees about the next meeting: the host of the meeting just past, the host of next month's meeting, the absentees themselves, or the presenter or leader for the next meeting. And then at each meeting, specifically say who is missing and establish who's going to call them, just to make sure it really does get done.

One serious issue that sometimes arises between meetings is that the chosen book may not be readily available. Solutions vary, according to the size of the group and the type of community you live in. Ann, for instance, says that for her group of eight women, people borrow the books from the local libraries, buy copies at garage sales, and even share or circulate copies (it helps that they're reading far in advance). Groups we talked to in Washington, D.C., and New York City had developed relationships with particular local bookstores that could order the books for everyone, if given a couple of weeks' time (one more reason for picking your books two months ahead!). Most independent bookstores will happily order books for a reading group, and may even give small discounts if the group is large enough.

Some groups insist that a book not be chosen unless they're sure it's available. This is sensible, though it does hamper the kind of inspired group-consensus selection process that some clubs love. Holly's book club decided to read Iris Murdoch's *An Unofficial Rose,* only to find that it was out of stock in most New York City bookstores. After a week or so of hunting for it, two members agreed over the phone to switch to Murdoch's *Bruno's Dream,* because three bookstores did have copies of that on the shelves. They thought they'd called everybody—maybe they did—but when meeting time rolled around, a couple of members had read *An Unofficial Rose,* not *Bruno's Dream,* and another person hadn't been able to find either book. Discussion was rather disjointed, to say the least.

When you do happen to see other members of your group between meetings, whether at work or socially, another subtle issue arises: Is it kosher to talk about the book outside of the meeting? "We all live in the same resort community [in Florida], and down here you usually see one another on the golf course or at bridge games, anyway," Ann says. "It's awfully difficult to keep your mouth shut when you see the reading group people beforehand. You want to talk about the book, but you know you've got to save it up for the meeting."

Denise agrees. "If I'm riding with somebody in a car to the group, it's an effort to keep from talking about the book beforehand," she admits. This reminds us a bit of being on jury duty: after the judge solemnly tells all the jury members that you're not allowed to talk about the case to one another during the trial, you sit together for hours in the jury room, trying like mad to avoid the topic that's uppermost in everyone's mind. It's another powerful testimony to how strangely important a book club is to its members. Nobody tells you that you can't talk about the book beforehand, but you don't, because you don't want to take the edge off the discussion. It matters to you.

# 4

# Chemistry Lessons

Every book group shares at least one peak experience—a meeting when everyone's juices are flowing at once and discussion builds from being absorbing to heated to electrifying to explosive. For our old group it happened with one of our most obscure choices—John Berger's *About Looking,* a series of essays about the politics of art appreciation. Berger makes no secret of his anti-bourgeois ideology, and this really annoyed half of the group—while the other half completely agreed with him. We'd been meeting for almost two years at this point, and we'd never before realized how different our political views were. Strangely, the book divided us absolutely along generational lines—the three who had been in college in the sixties were the pro-Berger faction and the three who hadn't entered college until the seventies were in the opposite camp. Maybe not so strange after all. Anyway, the discussion got very hot and also rather personal—if a couple of us hadn't stepped into the kitchen to cool off there's no telling *what* might have happened. Each member thumbed frantically through the text to cite passages to back up his or her position. The hours flew by as the cheese wilted untouched. Leaving the group that night, we all felt pretty beaten up mentally, but it was actually a good feeling—our heads were ringing with ideas, slogans, memories, and zippy comebacks we *should* have used. It had been a long time since we'd felt that stimulated. And, of course, we were all still friends at the next meeting.

Stephanie, a member of a long-running, all-women group in Denver, reports that their peak moment arrived the night they discussed Toni Morrison's *Beloved*: "It was one of the best meetings I ever remember having—and one of the greatest books I ever read. We have no black women in our group, but most are moms—and this book really hits deep in the issue of a mother's love. It was just a great discussion. As far as I'm concerned, the more powerful and intense the book the better the discussion."

Susan's lesbian/feminist book group has only been meeting a year, but they've already hit a peak together: "The book was *Lesbian Erotic Dance* by JoAnne Loulan, which examines the range of lesbian styles and choices. One woman in the group was obsessed with discussing sex. Every few minutes she kept saying, 'Okay, now, back to sex.' One of us finally said to her, 'I think you can let go of it now.' But no, she really wanted to talk about sex. We laughed but this was a really good discussion. We all took the most risks in revealing things about ourselves and how we viewed ourselves on the continuum from butch to femme. Usually, you have the book to hide behind, but this evening was great because no one hid. We were open and we took risks with what we had read and with our opinions. There was a lot of nervous laughter—but this meeting really cemented the group."

Hannah says that *Mating* by Norman Rush provoked one of the most emotional discussions in her otherwise rather prim and polite Seattle group: "It was a bitter discussion. Some women could not read the book—they refused to—or they started it and could not get through it, they hated it so much. Some were outraged by the presumption of a man writing in the voice of a woman. One camp said it was not believable or feminine. Another camp felt it was totally authentic, could have been one of us. One woman brought up the phrase: 'Wearing your tits down to the nub.' 'No woman would ever say that,' she kept insisting. So what if the narrator used one line that you did not agree with?—this did not contaminate the entire authenticity of the voice. The book brought out a lot of passion. I thought it was fabulous, others hated it. One woman got so upset by this discussion that when she got home she wanted her husband just to hold her—not to talk, just hold her."

What makes some book discussions incandesce while others only flicker? Although we have come up with no surefire formula for success, we do know of a number of ways to make conversation sparkle and avoid deadly silences (or bruising battles), and that's what this chapter is all about. Impassioned meetings are partly luck, partly chemistry—but effort and advance planning enter in as well. Members of successful book groups and book group advisors at major bookstores shared with us the ideas that have worked best for them.

## The Right Book

The choice of book is probably the most crucial ingredient in a successful meeting. "The books float the group," says Virginia Vallentine, book club advisor at Denver's mammoth Tattered Cover bookstore. "People get so excited by books. A good list is essential." For a book group, a "good" book is usually one that is controversial, packed with discussable issues, and likely to elicit strong opinions. Jane Smiley's *A Thousand Acres* is all of these—and, not surprisingly, it sparked memorable discussions in nearly all the book groups we talked to. Some members felt moved by the book to confess their own childhood experiences of incest or sexual abuse; some loved the book because it felt so real, so true to their own childhood memories; some hated it because the whole *King Lear* parallel felt too forced; other groups branched out from a discussion of the novel's style and character to a consideration of the economics of agriculture in the Reagan/Bush years.

Books that deal with gripping contemporary issues—gender relations, politics, race, religion, lifestyles, human rights—often provoke heated exchange. We sat in on one group the night they talked about *The Fatal Shore,* Robert

---

### A Few Dos and Don'ts to Guide

**Don't** choose self-help books. "They lie there and die," says one book club veteran. "The other problem is that they lead people to expose themselves. This can get dangerous—or tedious."

**Don't** stay too long with a single theme or genre. "My group almost died when we decided to spend a year just reading the Russians," one person comments. "The problem with narrowing your focus too much is that you feel like you're right back in school. Meetings have to be. fun." Our old group breathed a huge sigh of relief when we agreed that our project of plowing through all of Proust was *not* working. Variety is the spice of book groups.

**Do** choose books that at least one person in the group has already read and can vouch for. Some wonderful books do not lend themselves to discussion—and you should know this in advance.

Hughes's massive history of the settlement of Australia. Everyone agreed that the author's descriptions of the brutalities of the prison system were utterly chilling, though several members got bogged down in the long-winded, overly detailed narrative. The subject quickly shifted to prison conditions in America today: Were they really that much worse in Australia? Mary, who had just come back from Las Vegas, said the way women were turned into objects in the casinos reminded her of the total brutality and sexism toward women in Australia's early days, when women paraded around naked, bartering sex for survival. The group was off and running on

## Your Choice of Book

**Do** take chances. Don't rule anything out: You might have hated a certain author in college, but your taste may have changed in the interim. Or you might be surprised at how much you enjoy going back to an old favorite or reading some poetry for a change.

**Don't** be prissy. Let yourself be shocked. Roll with new ideas. As Virginia Vallentine says: *"Bastard Out of Carolina* is a very strong book and upset some groups—but that's what made the meetings good. The more able people are to open their minds and keep them open when they choose books and when they read, the better their reading will be and the better the groups will be."

**Do** make an effort to finish the book, no matter how much you loathe it. Discussions are always better when everyone in the group has read the book all the way through. If you hate it, finishing it will give you more ammunition.

an intense and sometimes sarcastic debate about sexism. Then the topic veered off into the rights of native peoples: Did the British treat Australia's aborigines any better than the American colonists treated the Native Americans? One woman member started to glorify aborigine culture but a man cut her off, reminding her that wife beating and infanticide were accepted practices. Nervous laughter. Finally someone interjected a question that silenced everyone else: "What would you do if you had been transported to Australia? Would you try to escape? Commit suicide?" And conversation swung from the abstract to the intensely personal, and so on, for another hour or so of lively, good-natured, if not totally focused, conversation.

Larry, whose Seattle-based all-male book group recently disbanded, recalls that one of their more gripping discussions was about a little-known history book entitled *Paris in the Terror* by Stanley Loomis. "It was a ponderous tome, but it dealt with a fascinating historical episode. There wasn't much to say about the book as literature, but discussion quickly branched off to the issue of individual rights. The men, several of whom are lawyers, illustrated their points with legal precedents while others brought in their own personal experiences."

Or take Norman Mailer's *The Executioner's Song*—a sprawling "true life" novel about murderer Gary Gilmore, who was executed in Utah in 1977. Mailer assembled the book by splicing together months of taped interviews with Gilmore and everybody connected with him. He gets totally inside Gilmore's head as he bounces in and out of prison, steals and kills and fools around with his girlfriend, and finally ends up on death row, resigned, even eager to be killed. Is this art or exploitation? Is a no-count desperado worth the 1,024 pages—and the Pulitzer Prize? Who got the royalties from this book? Can this legitimately be compared with Truman Capote's "nonfiction novel" *In Cold Blood*, or is Mailer doing something entirely different? Members differed— sometimes vociferously.

Of course, part of the chemistry comes in the reaction between book and book club members. As we discovered, the same book that ignites pyrotechnics in one group sometimes turns out to be a dud in others. Kyle's San Francisco men's group enjoyed *The Remains of the Day* by Kazuo Ishiguro, but he remembered this as one of their tamer evenings. "It was a good discussion but not very heated. We all agreed that the book was more Japanese than it was English. But we never really got beyond this." But Susan reports that the discussion of *The Remains of the Day* was totally incredible in her Denver feminist/lesbian group. "We all had such different reactions to the character and his choices. We all liked the beauty of the writing, but that was where the agreement ended. One woman said the butler needed therapy. Another had absolutely no compassion for this character: 'It's his problem' was her attitude. Others wanted to place the book in its historical context. There was this totally radical range of responses."

Most people we talked to agreed that a book does not have to be a literary gem to stir up debate and strong opinions. In fact, several groups reported that the most beautifully written, superbly crafted novels or nonfiction works turned out to be poor choices for discussion. Take *Madame Bovary:* in one group, the members were almost intimidated by this towering work of literary perfection. What was there to say that hadn't been said better by schools of French critics? Flaubert's letters proved to be a far better choice, with discussion ranging from Flaubert's relationship to his beloved *maman,* his bizarre love affair with Louise Colet, the role of love and friendship in a writer's life, and so on.

In another group, Alice Walker's *Possessing the Secret of Joy* fell flat: the women members agreed that it gave a harrowing picture of the barbaric practices women are subjected to, and they all loved the way the book was written—but the conversation never really got off the ground. The problem here was too much consensus.

Liza reports that all the members of her group admired *Friend of My Youth* by Alice Munro, but no one could think of much to say about it. She advises groups against choosing short stories. "For some reason, they just don't work. People jump from one story to another. It's harder to generalize. You fail to get into any depth." On the other hand, our own group had some absolutely wonderful meetings on short stories— *Dubliners* by James Joyce (lots of memories of Catholic childhoods), *Will You Please Be Quiet, Please?* by Raymond Carver (fierce debate, many passages read aloud to prove how wonderful or horrible Carver is), selections from Chekhov (the ultimate short story artist, humbling to read for all writers and hopeful writers).

For more ideas on books that have worked well in book clubs around the country, consult the annotated lists beginning on page 120.

## Don't Be Scared of a Good Fight

Vicki's group has been meeting regularly since the mid-sixties but the discussions remain as heated as ever—maybe more so. She attributes this in part to the members' relaxed, even encouraging attitude toward open combat. "We have no hard-and-fast rules," she says, "but no one minds fighting. There are sharp differences—that's what makes it good." The old adage about never discussing politics or religion at a dinner party does not apply to book groups. Anything goes. As Susan says of her Denver argumentative women-only group: "We wanted to get together a group of loud-mouthed opinionated women. We're all incredibly feisty. We differ. No one is afraid to say what they think. We call each other on things. We advance radical opinions."

Hannah feels that a couple of good brawls is exactly what

her Seattle women's book club needs to shake things up: "You can't say, 'This book sucks,'" she complains. "These women are afraid of 'gloves-off' stuff. We're polite at all costs. I resent having to conduct a polite discussion all the time." Eventually, the group called a special meeting just to discuss these sorts of problems. Discussions are still not as rough and bracing as Hannah would like, but at least *she* feels she can now be more forceful and direct without raising eyebrows.

Chris notes that one of the most memorable meetings of his Mercer Island couples book group was also one of the most vituperative. "I had chosen *Blood Meridian* by Cormac McCarthy and almost everyone hated it—passionately. It is a book written by someone with tremendous talent, yet people overlooked the writing and just reacted with abhorrence to the violence. Still, it provoked a good debate about violence—why it happens, why it is a continuing theme in history."

Controversy is good—but there can be too much of a good thing. Larry still cringes when he remembers the time he chose *The White Hotel* by D. M. Thomas. "Some of the guys were angry at me for having subjected them to something so offensive. I admit aspects of the book are hard to take. There is this passage in which the central female character is brutally murdered—it's just about the most horrifying thing I have ever read. But I warned them. I said, 'This book is a masterpiece— but it has one passage that is horrific.' Some of the guys were also stopped by the sexual content in the opening movement. The wife of one of the members was so offended that she threw the book in the garbage. The members could not see the qualities of the book—they refused to place its eroticism or violence in context. Their objections were not detailed or analytical enough to produce a rational discussion. They were so turned off that it killed the discussion."

One book club advisor regrets ever having recommended Margaret Atwood's *The Handmaid's Tale* to a group of middle-aged women. Three years later half the members are still not speaking.

One good rule we came across: *Don't* say flatly that you hated the book unless you're prepared to explain why. As one member says, "We had one woman who came and no matter what we had chosen she invariably said, 'I hated that book.' Nobody knew what to say and it stopped the discussion."

The bottom line here is: let the discussion get heated, even impassioned, but blow the whistle before debate degenerates into mudslinging. Stay with the issues. Don't get personal. And don't take things personally either. It's useful to develop a thick skin about your book choices and opinions. As one long-time book club member puts it, "If you pick a book you love, you get really invested in it and it becomes difficult when people criticize it. Remember—the group is not criticizing *you* but your book. Don't take it personally."

It may be helpful to address these issues head-on at your organizational meeting. Make it clear to everyone that the group will be a forum for honest discussion and debate and that harsh words may be exchanged. If you find that members are coming away from the meetings with hurt feelings, it may be time to call a kind of summit conference to address these interpersonal issues. Or read a book about anger management. For other ideas, see Chapter 6, our section about troubleshooting.

## Do You Need a Presenter?

Everyone agrees that if you want to get beyond the standard I-loved-it-I-hated-it gut reactions, then it's a good idea to come prepared—bring in your notes, jot down some questions, mark your favorite passages with Post-its, photocopy reviews. Sounds great in theory—but in practice, not everyone can be bothered. Many of us just don't read this way. It reminds us too much of all those dreary college courses—page after weary page highlighted in Day Glo yellow marker. Or we're too busy. Or we forget. Or we're convinced everyone will laugh.

Many groups we contacted have gotten around these objections by appointing one person at each meeting to be the presenter or facilitator. Virginia Vallentine, the group adviser at Denver's Tattered Cover bookstore, is a strong advocate of this system: "By all means have a presenter," she advises. "Group members should take turns. Each month, a different person should be responsible for getting together an author biography, doing some background research to put the book in perspective. But don't force it down their throats. And don't make the presentation too pedantic."

Kristin Kennell agrees wholeheartedly: "If you want your book club to work, someone *must* do outside research and lead the group. The presenter should not only offer a brief introduction but guide the discussion and offer his or her interpretation of the book. It is a good idea if the presenter—usually the person who has chosen the book—has already read it before it's recommended to the group. That way they know it's discussable and they can focus on the research."

We must confess that as we chatted with Kennell we felt a little icy pit opening up at the bottom of our stomachs: *So someone has to do a research project each month or the group will flop? A lecture? with footnotes? What are you supposed to do—take a leave of absence from your job or your family?* "It's really not that big a deal," she reassured us. "In most groups, the presentation on the author's life and times is about five to ten minutes." She points out that it helps if you know your way around the reference section of your local library. "A lot of people haven't been in a library in years. Some groups hold one of their meetings in a library. They chat with a librarian, find out where the research materials are. People are intimidated, but once they've done some research they see it isn't that hard. After your library meeting, reward yourselves by going out to a sinful dessert place."

In the groups we talked with, presentations ran the gamut from the five-minute once-over-lightly that Kennell described to a detailed exegesis delivered by a group member who felt truly inspired by a certain book. You'll know from the tone and style of your group where you should weigh in on this continuum. Most presenters perform two basic functions: first, they kick off discussion with a short speech about the major issues, reviews, biographical information; and then they take responsibility for keeping discussions on track, making sure all members have a chance to speak, curtailing lengthy digressions, and throwing out questions when the others run out of steam.

Some groups we talked to hire an outside person to lead discussions and in some cases choose the books they are going to read. This can get expensive, but many feel it's worth it because the quality of the discussion is so high. Other groups go with a paid presenter for a year or so, and then, once they get the hang of how to run a group, the members take over and do it themselves.

Cindy describes how she does research when it's her turn to lead: "I usually start by reading some reviews or author interviews. For example, when we did *A Thousand Acres,* I came across this interview in which Jane Smiley said how she had always hated *King Lear* but was also fascinated by it. The play bothered her because she felt it was misogynistic—she couldn't image how two women could treat their mad father like this. But it pricked her interest. She felt there had to be some explanation for this cruel treatment. So I described this interview to the group and it was a big help in focusing the discussion. It really got the dialogue started."

"Some years we've had a leader, some not," says Vicki of her Denver women's group. "When I'm leading I usually read the book twice and then spend a couple of hours in the library going over criticism. Then I speak for fifteen minutes or so. It's a kind of 'Great Books' approach. I ask questions about the major themes. I lead it as a discussion rather than a lecture. When things get too gossipy, the leader gets us back on track again. Having a leader centers us. If the leader takes the book seriously, then people read the book more attentively. When I'm leading, I like to remind the group to get back to the book instead of getting into tons of personal examples."

Vicki recalls one group meeting when the presenter really went to town: "Our group has one Jewish member and she chose *A Late Divorce* by A. B. Yehoshua. She is a brilliant woman and did an absolutely stunning presentation—it went on for two hours. She went through the book and analyzed the symbolism. She knew a lot about religious history and related this to the book, which was quite difficult and demanding. Everyone was glad it was not their turn—but we were mesmerized. I loved it."

This is truly rare. Most presenters take a far lower-key approach. Stephanie notes that when she leads the group, she tries to guide the discussion throughout the evening—but gently. "I do it in a way that's not real obvious. I will try to draw someone in, but not dramatically." It's become the custom in Stephanie's group for the leader to bring in a stack of photocopies of the most prominent reviews so everyone in the group can have one. In Liza's group the presenter may bring in visual materials—art of the period in which the book takes place or a travel book that conveys a feel for the place. There are endless variations on the basic theme.

Vivien Jennings, president of Rainy Day Books in Kansas City, has led a mothers and daughters and daughters-in-law group for about four years now and loves doing it. "I see myself as the guide," Jennings notes. "I keep the discussion tracking the book so we're not getting too far off the subject. We're always thinking and exploring. The discussions are very free-flowing, but I try to keep everyone from talking at once and I make sure one person doesn't dominate. I sometimes play devil's advocate just for the fun of it—just to keep them thinking."

When word spread of how successful this group is, other customers approached Jennings about leading their groups too, and the situation quickly got out of hand. "I can't lead all these groups, but I do help them get started," she says. "I'll meet with them the first time, recommend books, and show them how to do it—how to pick questions to get a discussion flowing and what sorts of topics to talk about. I tell them not to get too hot about things and not to get too personal. After this first meeting they can pretty much continue on their own, with each member taking a turn at leading the group." Jennings adds that if some of the members feel uncomfortable about leading, they shouldn't be made to do it: they can contribute by hosting the meetings instead while the other members do the presentations.

"A leader or facilitator can really help increase the group's understanding of the book and stretch their minds," Jennings believes. She recalls one evening when the book under discussion was *Possessing the Secret of Joy* by Alice Walker: "One woman came in and said to me at the start of the meeting, 'I liked this book, but I didn't think there was anything to it. Why were you so insistent that we read it?' I talked about the hidden agendas in the book and got the group to look one layer below at what was really going on. It turned out to be one of the most exciting—and loud—discussions we ever had. People were yelling about women's issues and the subliminal ways that women are kept in their place in this society. At the end my ears were ringing. As we were leaving I turned to this skeptical woman and said, 'So? Do you still think there was nothing to discuss in this book?' "

If you decide not to go with a presenter or facilitator, it still makes sense for someone to come prepared with a few leading questions or comments to get the ball rolling. Usually this falls to the person who has chosen the book or who is hosting the meeting. You might start by explaining why you picked this particular title or isolate a couple of themes you'd like to talk about. We never used a presenter in our old group, but Adele frequently had read a biography of the author and brought in her copy of the book so we could flip through it and look at the pictures. When discussions flagged, she would always introduce some curious facts about the author's life, and we'd be off and running again.

One member said that her group never appointed a leader or facilitator, but they have a kind of unwritten rule that the person with the strongest feelings about the book jumps in

---

## Ten Good Questions to Get Discussion Going

1. What do you think the title means?
2. Why do you think the author opened the book this way?
3. Did the jacket copy give you a fair idea of what the book would be like?
4. What other books that the group has read could this one be compared to?
5. How autobiographical do you think this book is?
6. Are the male or the female characters more vividly and fully drawn?
7. Why has the author chosen this particular narrator? Can you imagine this story told in a different voice?
8. Under what conditions did various members read the book (all in one sitting, short hits each night at bedtime, on the train, etc.)? Was this a good or bad way to read it?
9. Did this book make you want to read anything else by the same author? Why or why not?
10. Who in hell picked this one and why?

first and leads the discussion. This works fine as long as the book elicits strong opinions.

It helps if you try to vent your feelings in a way that will get people talking. Say you're discussing *The Age of Innocence* and you feel it's one of the best things you've read in years. Instead of just gushing, "Wasn't this fabulous? I just couldn't put it down," you might try opening with something like: "Can you imagine what this story would be like if Wharton were writing it now? Do you think these elements could be translated into the present—or was the entire situation shaped by the age that the characters lived in?"

Kristin Kennell recommends jotting down a few "What if? . . ." questions about each title: What if the father died instead of the mother? What if the wife found out about the adultery? What if the sister had never gone to Nicaragua? And, when all else fails, you can always talk about how you would cast (or recast) the movie version.

## "Doing" the Book

Over and over, book club members griped to us that they left their meetings feeling that they hadn't really "done" the book. Discussion ended before they got to the heart of the matter. Or it focused entirely on the characters and failed to get at the author's intent. Or they talked about the themes but neglected the style and structure of the book.

Other people told us that they'd love to start a book group but they worry that, as amateurs, they wouldn't be able to do a book justice. We recommended finding a presenter, but they worried that this would entail too much of a commitment.

The following list should help. If your discussion touches on at least these six areas, you can rest assured that you have "done" the book in a thorough and satisfying way.

**Context and background.** When did the author live? What other books and intellectual movements were in the air then? What is the book's place in literary history? What is its place in the author's career? Answering these questions is much more important when you're reading a classic or a book from a foreign country or culture, but they will enrich the discussion of every book.

**Meaning of the text.** The meaning of any literary text is open to endless interpretation, but some books are more difficult to interpret than others. The meaning of Willa Cather's *My Ántonia,* say, is crystal clear compared with William Faulkner's *The Sound and the Fury.* You can launch into your discussion of meaning by talking about plot: Does everyone know more or less what happened in the book? Or, if it's impossible to say what happened, why is it so obscure? Then move on to authorial intent: What was the author trying to do with this book—entertain? Reform society? Exorcise personal demons? Can you identify any messages—political, moral, social—that the author was trying to get across?

**Content.** What new things did you learn from reading this book? With nonfiction, especially history, biography, or journalism, the discussion of content may occupy most of the meeting. With fiction, you could talk about what the book is *really* about—which often merges with the meaning of the text. You may find yourselves gossiping about the characters as if they were your friends—this is another crucial aspect of content.

**Technique.** You can start by trying to describe the author's style and discussing whether or not it works. How would you describe the author's "voice"? What sort of dialogue does the author use? Is the prose style very flowery and rhetorical or stripped down to bare essentials? What role do symbols and metaphors play? What about the book's structure: How does the plot work? How does it hang together? Does the story have a satisfying beginning, middle, and end?

**Appreciation.** Here's where a reading group differs from a college English class: it's perfectly okay to say you didn't like a book choice, or to say you loved it even if it's not "great" literature. You can also relate to the book on a gut level—how did it make you feel? Compare it to other books you've read, especially books you've read with the book group.

**Anecdotes.** Smaller and more intimate groups often enjoy exchanging memories, dreams, and reflections inspired by the book. Stories from childhood, tales of eccentric friends and relatives, travel impressions, even descriptions of where and when you read this book—all are fair game in book groups, just so long as you relate it back to the work at hand.

## Let the Discussion Wander—
## But Not Too Far

Fran is thinking about dropping out of her group. It was organized out of the local branch of one of the big chain bookstores and run by an English professor at a nearby community college. The problem is the professor—let's call her Shirley. Shirley moderates the group with an iron fist. Let the discussion stray even a hair from strict, abstract literary analysis and Shirley blows the whistle. Just recently the group read some Peter Taylor short stories. An African-American housecleaner figured prominently in one of the stories. A group member, herself African-American, brought up the question of how members of her race are portrayed in the works of white Southern writers. "Take Faulkner, for example . . ." she began, only to be cut off in midstream by Shirley's whistle. "Let's bring it back to the subject at hand," Shirley said sweetly but firmly. "Now, we were talking about Taylor's use of an unreliable narrator, weren't we?"

No wonder Fran wants to quit. Successful book groups are emphatically *not* college seminars. They live and breathe on informality, free-wheeling discussion, quirky digression, and humor. One essential lesson is to let discussion wander where it will—as long as it doesn't wander totally off the map or back into the same old groove.

Hannah gives us an example of an amusingly erratic discussion from her group: "For some reason we were reading this Buddhist tract called *Miracle of Mindfulness*—a manual on meditation. What can you say about meditation? You certainly can't criticize it. This whole subject was so far from our lives. And yet despite this odd choice of book, some good topics came up. One woman asked: 'Are you allowed to have any fun in Buddhism?' Somehow this got another member going about how she lost her virginity at the age of twenty-seven. This was very funny."

Chris tells us about a fierce series of digressions prompted by Cristina García's novel *Dreaming in Cuban*: "No one thought it was a great book, but nonetheless the discussion got really far afield and very intense. Several members picked up on the book's treatment of the *santería* cult and the surrealistic religious elements in the book. This provoked a discussion about religion and culture that got quite testy. One guy from India pointed out that our dismissive remarks about the goat sacrifice reflected our upper-middle-class orientation and our cultural myopia. Then someone asked whether religion was just a cultural construct. And someone else asked if anyone in the group had had a religious experience. There were several confessions, each of which was critiqued in turn. The three shrinks in the group started accusing the rest of us of glorifying science. Somehow we wandered from religion to particle physics. One of the shrinks started going on about quantum theory and the uncertainty principle. I let him have it on this one, pointing out that this had nothing to do with the basic question under discussion, which was whether or not religion was a system of culturally shaped beliefs. The uncertainty of science is totally different from the uncertainty of religion. And so on. Six or seven of us really got wound up. The group didn't break up till after midnight!"

On the other hand, we heard of one New York City group in which a member—always the same member—always grabs the floor and starts yakking about whatever pops into her mind: current events, vacation plans, anecdotes about her past. Her ramblings relate only tangentially to the book. Once she gets going, the other members become irritated and restless, and usually the evening breaks up before the book discussion is really over. This group would probably benefit from having a presenter to keep the discussion on track. For more solutions to the problem of overly personal digressions, see Chapter 6.

A single person can ruin a book discussion by talking too much or getting too far off the topic—but an individual can also spoil the meeting by remaining utterly silent. A person who says nothing is like a black hole, sucking in energy from everybody else. It makes the others uncomfortable. Book groups should have a rule that every member should say *something* each meeting, even if they think it sounds dumb. If you haven't finished the book, comment on the beginning. Or ask a searching question.

## Call In an Expert

"It can really help start a good discussion if one member of the group has some expertise or some life experience that pertains to the work at hand," notes Larry. "This can illuminate the book in interesting ways. In my old group we read *Jurassic Park* one month. One guy is a zoologist, a professor at the University of Washington. So we all turned to him and asked, 'So what about the science in this book? Is it on target?' Steve talked at length about his own work on evolutionary biology. It was a neat angle on the book."

Debby, in our old group, went through a heavy Latin American phase, learning Spanish and traveling to Mexico, Nicaragua, and Costa Rica. She totally sprang to life the night we discussed *Under the Volcano* and gave us some eye-opening pictures of what Mexican cantinas are actually like and what happens on the Day of the Dead. Similarly, Stephanie who had served as a tour guide at a local exhibit of Egyptian art, became her group's resident expert during the discussion of Mailer's *Ancient Afternoons*. And Chris mentions that the three psychiatrists in his couples book group often provide an interesting Freudian perspective on literature. "The shrinks really had a field day with Margaret Atwood's *Cat's-Eye*," he says. "The book concentrates on childhood and lends itself to a Freudian interpretation. It was a psychiatric evening, shall we say."

Special expertise is fine, but beware of know-it-alls or dogmatic boors or uptight professionals. Kristy, a lawyer, had fresh insights and lively views on Saul Bellow and Mark Twain. But when the group decided to go for a spellbinding contemporary novel and chose Scott Turow's *Presumed Innocent,* she lectured everyone obnoxiously on how the law *really* works. Mary, who has a masters in French literature, stifles conversation with her unbearable Gallic haughtiness whenever discussion strays into anything French.

What about reading a book written by one of the group members or inviting the author to a discussion? The book group people we talked to had mixed feelings about this. Our New York book group had several published authors, but we all felt that it would be a bad idea to choose one of their books for discussion: What if we all hated it? Or asked embarrassing intimate questions? Or suspected that we were the basis for any of the characters? We've heard of groups that serve as workshops for analyzing and criticizing the members' writing—but these are a different breed from book groups.

Our own feeling is that discussing a book by one of the members is just too risky—unless you're all fed up with the group and looking for a way to self-destruct. A better idea is to invite a guest speaker now and then who has some expertise in the works of the author you have read.

# 5

## Moveable Feasts

For the first five or so years our old reading group met, we had a lot of fun serving refreshments that were somehow appropriate for the book we were reading. When we read two plays by August Strindberg, we munched on Swedish meatballs. For our meeting on Darwin's *The Origin of Species* (dreadful discussion—what a tedious book), Linda gave us each our own little box of animal crackers. When we read John Le Carré's *The Spy Who Came in from the Cold,* it was scotch whisky, served straight up, while four of us sat at a kitchen table under a low-hanging light, as though we were under interrogation in a safe house. We didn't have much to say about the book, so we played a great drunken game of Scrabble instead.

Perhaps our group's greatest drink coup was when we read *Under the Volcano,* Malcolm Lowry's searing novel about an alcoholic British consular officer in provincial Mexico. Dan managed to get hold of a bottle of mescal, the consul's favorite potent liquor—authentic down to the worm in the bottom of the bottle.

But the most memorable moment in the entire history of

the reading group was probably the night we met to discuss *Swann's Way,* the first volume of Marcel Proust's *Remembrance of Things Past.* Naturally, Debby had gone to a French bakery in the neighborhood and bought madeleines, those exquisite little tea cakes that Proust said brought back with one bite a flood of memories of his childhood. Paul, picking up a madeleine, said, "Watch this." He bit in, his eyes bulged, and he let out a primal scream. And after years of hearing Paul complain about his family, we all knew exactly what he meant to convey. We laughed so hard that our faces and rib cages hurt for the rest of the evening.

Because our group always put so much thought into the foods we served at our meetings, we were surprised to find out that most book clubs don't. Just about every group does have some kind of refreshment, of course, even if it's only coffee. The majority of clubs meet on weekday nights, and many members come to the meeting straight from their offices, so some sustenance is required. And since most clubs meet in people's houses, there's a feeling that the host ought to offer his or her guests *something.* But food isn't (and shouldn't be) a major focus of attention.

Several people we talked to, though, admit that it's essential, especially in the women's groups. "Food helps to relax people, and it helps them make the transition from their day into the book discussion," points out one member of a book club of writers, editors, and journalists.

"Do you think women ever get together without something to eat?" another book club member said wryly to us. "Food is all important—you know women and food," echoed another female reader of a totally different generation, different part of the country, and different sexual orientation.

Maybe book clubs that deliberately downplay food do so to assert that they are "serious," not just social. They're missing a wonderful opportunity, though, in our humble opinion. The great thing about a reading group is that it *is* both serious and social, and it binds a group of readers together in personal as well as intellectual ways. So why not enjoy feeding the body as well as the mind?

## Grazing, Salty or Sweet

In our old reading group, the custom was to serve nibbling food, rather than a full meal. Since our meetings started at eight P.M., presumably we'd all had time to catch dinner beforehand. In practice, however, nobody bothered to have dinner on those nights because we'd be well fed at the meeting. (You *can* make a meal on cheese and crackers, if you gobble enough Gouda.) We should probably have gone ahead and done dinner, but once the pattern was laid down, nobody made an effort to change it.

If your group does decide to go the snacks-and-appetizers route, cheese and crackers is a perennial favorite. If there's a good store in the neighborhood where you can buy imported cheeses, you may even sometimes be able to serve a cheese that matches the book—Stilton when you read Dickens, Camembert for *Madame Bovary,* or Danish blue cheese when you read Isak Dinesen.

Cheese can get awfully boring, though. For variety, try serving sushi, provided you know a good place to get it absolutely fresh, or a platter of fat boiled shrimp with a red cocktail sauce on the side. Cut-up raw vegetables, served with a tangy dip, is another good and healthy alternative, though it does require a little more preparation time.

Salted nuts, pretzels, taco chips, and potato chips are obvious options, inexpensive and easy to pick up at the last minute. In the excitement of book discussion, however, people may end up eating more of these than they realize, and then they'll get awfully thirsty—make sure you have enough cold drinks on hand.

Several other groups that we talked to just serve dessert or some sort of sweets. This can range all the way from, as one woman in an all-women group described it, "Hershey's Kisses in a cut-glass bowl" to "Spiffy-looking desserts and silver spoons all lined up," as another woman described the usual offerings at her Friday-evening book club of couples. The emphasis is usually on something rich, gooey, and indulgent, a treat that the individual group members would rarely allow themselves on their own. Coffee and tea are always offered with the dessert, and often soft drinks as well.

The virtue of desserts is that the host can usually pick up something at a bakery on the way home the day of the meeting, although as one Denver reading group member told us, "I bake when it's at my house, and another woman in the group had apple crisp for us. It's so female."

In these cases, the members definitely do eat dinner beforehand (surviving the evening on one slice of chocolate mousse cake is not very feasible). Some groups, however, drink wine or beer during the book discussion, then wind up the evening with dessert.

## The Meal Deal

One New York City group, all women, decided at the outset to gather over a meal each time—as one member, a veteran of another group, pointed out, "there is something civilizing about breaking bread together." After nearly two years, the group had grown to ten people (when all showed up) and they reevaluated the idea of serving dinner, since cooking for such a large group was more of an obligation than feeding six or seven. Brown-bagging was suggested as an alternative. But in the end, they decided to stick with the plan of having each month's host cook the meal. "Yeah, it *is* more difficult to cook a meal for ten people," one member articulates it, "but then, with more people in the group, you end up having to host the thing less often. When you look at it that way, cooking the one big dinner doesn't seem so onerous. And the pleasure of sitting down together over a good meal was worth it."

On the other hand, a man we spoke to who was "shopping around" for a book club decided not to join a particular group in large part because dinner was included. "It's hard enough getting dinner for my own family," he groaned to himself. Others complained to us that food started out as a sideshow at their book groups and eventually took over center stage. The more time and effort members spent on preparing meals, the less they devoted to the book discussion. In one group, in Ithaca, New York, the members decided to make this change of direction official: the group has become a cookbook club, with members whipping up elaborate monthly meals from obscure cookbooks and then sharing the recipes. Sometimes they tie in with relevant literature— Chekhov stories for a Russian feast, Derek Walcott for Caribbean curries, that kind of thing. The members who were more interested in reading than eating dropped out.

Serving dinner for a book group *can* work, but it's absolutely essential to keep it in perspective. The cardinal rule is: Book discussion always comes first. The host should not spend forty minutes in the kitchen while the others are talking about the book, nor should other members be drafted into chopping, stirring, or basting duties. And the meal should not be so impressive that everyone at the table talks about it instead of the book. Two courses is the limit, and even that should be optional.

Whether or not your group can successfully have dinner at your meetings will depend on a number of factors—size, for one thing. If more than twelve people regularly come to your meetings, it'll be hard to fit everybody around a dining room table. It also depends on whether you've got a lot of fussy eaters in the group. If a club had several people with dietary restrictions, choosing a menu month after month would no

## No-Frills Eats

A book club is not a one-time commitment—you'll be meeting month after month, presumably for years, or at least you hope so when you're starting out. So if your group does decide to meet over a meal, make sure you keep it simple enough and casual enough that hosting doesn't begin to seem a chore. How?

- Serve buffet-style rather than sit-down meals.

- Consider using paper plates and plastic cups. Although it's not environmentally correct, look at it this way—you'll save water and energy by not running a dishwasher.

- Serve foods that are easily eaten with a fork off a plate held in the lap, so you don't have to worry about seating everyone around a dining room table. Moving from one room to another can interrupt or limit the time allotted for book discussion, anyway.

- Stress how important it is for every member to RSVP before a meeting, so that the host has an accurate head count and doesn't have to cook a lot of food that goes uneaten.

doubt be impossible. (One of us comes from a family that includes two vegetarians, one non-cheese-eater, and one non-egg-eater, so we know what it's like to plan around what foods people will eat.)

People whose lives are really hectic may elect to do the simplest (and most expensive) thing, which is to hire a small room in a local restaurant for their book club meetings and have everyone simply order whatever they want to eat during the discussion. We've heard of a couple of groups who do this. One of them circulates to different restaurants each time; the other always meets in the same local Chinese restaurant, where the staff has learned just how to handle their needs. (Luckily, everybody in that group likes Chinese food.)

The Cornell alumni book club in New York City meets at the Cornell Club, which has a full kitchen and restaurant. An optional buffet is laid out for book club meetings—nothing elaborate, just "munchie foods," sandwiches, and salads—and anyone who goes to the buffet is charged fifteen dollars on his or her club account, which isn't too bad a deal. It's simple and it's optional, though it's not universally popular. "A lot of people think maybe we should just bag the food—there are people that like that food and others that don't," a member of the group tells us. In general this group has a lot of casual drop-in members, who may only show up for one or two meetings, so having the meetings at the club means that nobody has to commit to hosting the meeting. It may be, however, that this lower degree of commitment will weaken the group in the long run.

Since most reading groups meet in members' homes, agreeing to feed the whole crowd every month requires the commitment of every member in his or her turn. The burden has to be shared equally. Three groups that we talked to faced the situation of several members moving out of the immediate area but still wanting to stay in the group. These emigrating members took to "hosting" the meeting at another member's home, which meant that they had to somehow bring in the food they were serving, even a full dinner. Still, they manage to do it, in order to maintain their status as fully functioning book club members.

A group has to be willing to tolerate different levels of entertaining style. If competition sets in over who can cook the most elaborate meal, hosting will become a chore for everyone. If a group starts heading in this direction, the best thing you could do would be to simply order in pizzas next time it's your turn. Or announce that you're using canned sauce on the pasta, or that the soup was made from a packet. Make a virtue of your laziness and your lack of pretension, and others can feel free (*whew!*) to take the cue from you.

The meals should be casual—casseroles, chili, quiche, etc.—the kinds of foods that ladies used to serve at bridge club luncheons when ladies used to have time to give luncheons in their homes. ("Tea and comfort food," as one Denver-area member describes it.) *The Joy of Cooking* cookbook has a whole chapter devoted to these brunch and luncheon dishes. Foods that can be cooked ahead of time and quickly reheated—turkey tetrazzini or a simple lamb stew— are lifesavers for working people. Main course salads are great if you can make them the night before and serve them cold or at room temperature (look in *The Silver Palate Cookbook* under "Significant Salads"). Hearty soups are a good and easy option, served with crusty rolls or breads and maybe a crisp salad. Wendy, in a women's group in New York City, says she can practically still taste the amazing soup with crème fraiche on top that one member of her group served one month.

Think ethnic too—curries, stir fries, pastas, tacos, moussaka—for well-balanced, filling, one-dish meals. If there's a good ethnic restaurant in your neighborhood that delivers, so much the better. It's great if this coincides with a month when you've all read a book from that country, but don't wait for that opportunity.

## Brown-Bag and Potluck

A woman in Portland, Oregon, told us that her group, which meets at lunchtime, used to have a fairly elaborate meal served. After a while, it just got to be too much, and now they all happily brown-bag it. Rebecca's New York City group took the same tack in order to simplify food matters when several members moved to the suburbs. "Just this year we changed it so that now it's strictly a brown-bag deal," she said. "The host provides drinks and that's it."

Brown-bag means that each person brings his or her own food, and inevitably there's a bit of peeking over to see what everybody else brought, which can be fun or can be distracting. Another alternative is potluck—having each member bring one thing to contribute to the group repast. Potluck is nice in theory, but it has to be carefully organized, with different people "assigned" parts of the meal (and that sort of defeats the idea of potluck, doesn't it?). Although potluck does take the onus off the host for providing food for everybody, on the other hand it requires everyone to bring something every month.

And people can start to get lazy about potluck. Left to themselves to contribute whatever, the members of Denise's Washington, D.C., book club end up just picking up something packaged and quick on the way from the office. As a result, the refreshments at their meetings tend to be a strange combinations of wine, soda, salty high-fat snacks, and calorie-laden sweets—which of course they promptly devour. Nobody has complained though, Denise says. Maybe it just reminds them of being back at college.

## Logistics

Snacks or desserts can simply be set on little tables around the living room, but when you're serving a full meal, it's a logistical event. In one Seattle group, the dinner is often prepared during the meeting, while members mill around drinking beer. In practice, this often means that once they finally get to the table, only a small amount of time is spent on discussing the book. A prospective member was really turned off by this.

Both Brad's and Wendy's New York City groups have cocktail hour first, then when they sit down to eat, it's a cue that it's time to discuss the book. This has the considerable virtue of making sure that they'll talk about the book for at least as long as it takes to eat.

This is no small benefit. Another group we talked to got into the habit of talking about the book during cocktail time, then adjourning to the dining room or kitchen to get dinner. Even if they came right back to the living room and ate off plates on their laps, they somehow couldn't get the book talk going again. It's a problem they're still working on, though like many book club problems, it's ticklish to address head-on, since certain personalities are involved. Members have discussed this pattern individually outside of meetings, however, and try hard each meeting to steer the straying discussion back on track.

If your group rotates moderator duties, it may seem logical to expect each month's host to act as moderator too (it's certainly easier to keep track of who's responsible). But if a full meal is being served, it may be too much for one person to handle all at once—either the dinner won't be served up right, or the discussion will falter when the cook gets up to check on the food in the oven. Consider instead doing what one group we talked to does: have hosts chosen by a regular rotation system, and then let other people in the group volunteer to be moderators, according to how interested they are in the upcoming book. Or do as one all-couples group we spoke to does: each time a couple hosts the meeting, one spouse is responsible for moderating, while the other is responsible for refreshments. The next time it's that couple's turn, the spouses switch duties.

## Booze or Not?

This may be a question that gets raised at your first organizational meeting, especially if some people are anxious to
make sure there *isn't* any alcohol served. But more likely,
your own group's preferences will just evolve. Whatever is
served at the first meeting will probably set a pattern for several meetings, but if hardly anybody ever touches the liquor,
people will start to take note, and gradually they won't bother
to have it on hand when they're hosts. If lots of people ask for
diet cola at one meeting, next month's host would be smart to
remember to have some on hand too. Gradually, you get to
know what people in your group drink.

And then, of course, their tastes change. At our group's
early meetings, almost everyone had either beer or wine to
drink, and sometimes even scotch or a gin and tonic. By the
time we'd been meeting for ten years, though, herbal tea, coffee and seltzer were more popular. Perhaps it's no coincidence that during that same time period, three members of
the group quit smoking—by the end, Paul was our sole
smoker, and even he forbore lighting up for the duration of
the meeting.

Many groups we talked to said that alcohol—usually
wine—is routinely served at their meetings, but there isn't a
lot of drinking going on. In all our interviews we only heard
of one instance of someone getting stinking drunk at a
meeting—and she was a guest who was never invited back.
One long-term group told us that they used to drink a lot
more back in the early sixties; now the twelve of them rarely
finish a single bottle of wine. Heavy boozing has gone out of
fashion at book clubs as much as at business lunches.

Several people suggested that members don't drink because they want to keep their heads clear for book discussions. But on the flip side, one book club member we talked
to said, "I can definitely get more passionate about the book
after having a few glasses of wine . . . One book that totally

blew me away was *Possession: A Romance* [by A. S. Byatt], and after a couple of glasses, I made everybody read aloud parts of the poems in it. Then I made David read some more aloud, 'cause he's got this beautiful reading voice." This kind of rapturous response to the book is the sort of thing none of us were allowed to do in college English classes (you couldn't drink during class either, at least not at the colleges we went to). And isn't that why most of us join book clubs—so that we can read books with a less academic, more personal response?

As with food, keeping the drink choices simple is important. Offering a fully stocked bar for mixed drinks is fine, if you always keep your bar fully stocked anyway, but who wants to be a bartender in his or her own home?

Wine is a popular choice, maybe because it can satisfy both serious drinkers and occasional drinkers. Wine also has a certain sort of upscale cultural connotation, which somehow goes along with literary evenings. The downside of wine is that you can open a nice bottle of chablis for one person, and then have no other takers. The bottle ends up recorked in the back of your refrigerator, waiting to be used for cooking. This is less of a problem if you're serving dinner—more people are likely to take at least some wine during the meal.

A good rule of thumb would be one bottle of wine for every three people you expect to come. If you offer both red and white wine, buy enough of each to serve everybody at the meeting, just in case everybody asks for the same color. After all, an unopened bottle of wine will always get used (even if you don't drink it, you can take it along as a gift next time you get invited to someone's house for dinner).

If you have a sizeable contingent of beer drinkers in your group, serving beer is awfully handy. There's less waste, since you only have to open one beer bottle at a time, and if people drink straight from the bottle or can, you may be able to get away with fewer glasses to wash afterward. Since beer should be served cold, though, you may have to clean out your refrigerator to make room for several six-packs. And if you're not a beer drinker yourself, you don't want to get stuck with a refrigerator full of Heinekens.

Other liquor choices are fun occasionally (we all sampled Dan's *Under the Volcano* mescal, though once was certainly enough). Stephanie's Denver women's group sometimes serves margaritas along with the Mexican food—burritos, nachos, green chiles—that all the members like. And when Brad's New York City group read a Dashiell Hammet mystery one month, it seemed absolutely fitting for them to drink scotch with it.

We're always surprised at how quickly the club soda or seltzer water disappears at all the meetings we go to—people don't focus on fizzy water as a drink of choice, but it's always a safe alternative for those who don't like alcohol, or don't like caffeine, or don't like calories, or don't like artificial sweeteners. And it's also an all-purpose mixer—with liquor, with wine, with fruit juices. So our advice to anyone who's hosting is: Buy lots of seltzer.

## Special Occasions

If food is not a large component of your group's regular meetings, you still might have occasional meetings where the host serves a memorable treat or where you all sit down to dinner together. Judy's Cambridge, Massachusetts, reading group usually meets in town, near the hospital where several members work, but they look forward to meeting in summer out at Rick's house in the suburbs, because he has a swimming pool. Although their usual meeting food is simple snacks, Rick's wife is a gourmet cook and likes to lay out a fabulous spread for them. Everyone is happy for this occasional variation on the routine.

For a change, Denise's reading group of writers in Washington, D.C., picked *A Tale of Two Cities* to read for a meeting that happened to fall on Bastille Day, and they held their meeting at a French restaurant. "It was kind of distracting, but fun," Denise remembers. Afterward, they decided that they'd like to try meeting at local cafés again from time to time.

Another group we talked to—an all-women group that serves only snacks at their regular meetings—has developed a tradition of having a big potluck dinner together around Christmas time. They don't invite guests, not even their spouses, to this dinner, and they have a great time every year.

Our old group had two such traditions: we tried to spend a Saturday night together every summer at Adele's house upstate (this got even easier after Dan and Debby found a weekend house up the road from Adele's) and we usually served a birthday cake at the October meeting, the anniversary of the group's first meeting.

In Chapter 6 we'll suggest various kinds of special outings reading groups can enjoy together, but the idea of an annual book club dinner is a ritual in its own right. This could be at a restaurant; it could be catered; it could be potluck. Tie it in to some book that you're reading, and you have a memorable occasion that will bind the group together.

## Great Book Meals

Matching food to books is fun, but don't get too hung up on it. After all, if your group reads mostly nineteenth- and twentieth-century American and British novels, as the majority of groups do, you could end up eating either turkey and cornbread or roast beef and mashed potatoes at every other meeting. And lots of writers (we hate to say it, but especially male writers) pay so little attention to food in their books that you'd be stumped for menu inspirations. At the other end of this spectrum are contemporary writers who lace their prose with brand names—imagine a meal consisting of nothing but Cheetos, Hawaiian Punch, Ring Dings, and Swanson TV dinners. It could happen.

But there are some books that cry out for special meals to accompany them. Here are a few:

*A Year in Provence* by Peter Mayle (207 pp.) Mayle's humorous account of the characters and escapades of his first year in Provence is a rather lightweight reading choice, but you can get into the sybaritic spirit with a feast of Provençal food, such as a pungent ratatouille (eggplants, zucchini, tomatoes, sweet peppers, and onions stewed together with a drizzle of olive oil). Make sure of course that you have lots of crusty bread, ripe soft cheeses, and robust red wine.

*The Leopard* by Giuseppe di Lampedusa (320 pp.) Written by a Sicilian nobleman, this spellbinding 1958 novel is set in the Garibaldian political upheavals of the 1860s, centered on an aristocratic family facing the end of its class's reign. Lampedusa's sensual, vivid descriptions of provincial Sicily could be enhanced by a heaping platter of pasta tossed with olives, toasted pine nuts, chopped plum tomatoes, and basil.

*The Joy Luck Club* by Amy Tan (332 pp.) Interweaving stories of the lives of four Chinese immigrant women and their American-born daughters, Tan's first novel is the sort of book that resonates the more you talk about it. Order in a Chinese banquet from a local restaurant, or make your own cold sesame noodles, sweet-and-sour soup, and Buddha's delight (stir-fried mixed vegetables over rice).

*Brideshead Revisited* by Evelyn Waugh (351 pp.) The upper-crust world of Sebastian Flyte and Charles Ryder is quintessential Masterpiece Theater England, from Oxford to the country manor house to deb party London. One of Waugh's least jaundiced books (far better than the poisonously bitter *A Handful of Dust*), it's a perfect opportunity to serve high tea: cucumber sandwiches, toasted scones and jam, tiny fruit tarts, and slices of frosted cake. Wash it down with Earl Grey tea or dry sherry.

*Lonesome Dove* by Larry McMurtry (843 pp.) Get into the spirit of McMurtry's epic cattle drive novel by serving up chuckwagon food: baked beans topped with bacon, chile con carne, thin-sliced bread toasted hard, and apple pie with coffee.

*Fried Green Tomatoes at the Whistle-Stop Cafe* by Fannie Flagg (403 pp.) Two counterpointed plots show us two absorbing friendships—one of a pair of young women in the Depression-era Deep South, the other of a feisty couple of modern-day older women. The younger women's story is set in the café mentioned in the title, and plenty of menu suggestions pop up—try some fried chicken with mashed potatoes and cream gravy.

*Between Meals: An Appetite for Paris* by A. J. Leibling (185 pp.) An American master of prose style, Leibling spent a year in Paris in the 1920s before joining the staff of *The New Yorker,* and this nostalgic book brings to life the magic of that era. Since Leibling's great discovery in Paris was gourmet food, you'll appreciate the book better if you feast on fresh oysters on the half shell; onion soup topped with melted cheese and a crouton; pâté on French bread; and a chocolate souffle for dessert. Choose excellent French wines, and don't omit a final cognac.

*Spartina* by John Casey (375 pp.) In this understated novel, Casey unsentimentally conjures up the dreams, loves, and fears of an ordinary working man: Dick Pierce, a down-on-his-luck fisherman in coastal Rhode Island. Serve shrimp, fresh farm-stand tomatoes, beer, and blueberry buckle, to bring a salty whiff of sea air into your meeting.

*Like Water for Chocolate* by Laura Esquivel (245 pp.) Imagine Gabriel García Marquez as a woman who relishes all things culinary, and you'll have a sense of the flavor of this Mexican novel about three sisters at the turn of the century. The narrator's great-aunt Tita was a born cook and the tales are spun from her beloved cookbook, complete with recipes. The stew of corn, chilis, raisins, and cinnamon sounds irresistible. After feasting, compare the book to the movie.

# 6

# Troubleshooting

For years our book group hummed along smoothly with lively discussions, deepening ties among the members, and a list of books chosen that everyone read eagerly and happily. We spent a rainy weekend talking about *Adam Bede* at Adele's country house. *Nostromo* by Joseph Conrad surprised us by how vividly cinematic it was. Linda knew Walter Abish and enlivened our meeting on his eerie novel *How German Is It?* with gossip and anecdotes. We hung in there for *Moby-Dick*. *Billy Phelan's Greatest Game* by William Kennedy was an unexpected favorite.

But then, gradually but inexplicably, things began to go sour. Attendance grew sparse and erratic. Linda's health problems eventually made her drop out. David moved to the suburbs and had twins and complained he was too exhausted to finish the books or drag into the city. When Paul, whose sense of humor always delighted us, began working nights and pretty much stopped coming, the group hardly ever laughed anymore. The remaining members hated ill-informed book choices like *Mohawk* by Richard Russo and *Foxybaby* by Elizabeth Jolley. We didn't really know what to say about Robert

Burns's poems. We had more and more trouble deciding which book to read, and when we did meet, few of us had bothered to finish the book. The meetings became more and more of a chore. We tried to institute a new system—one "big" book to be read for quarterly meetings and smaller books for the months in between, but it didn't really work. The group dwindled down to three or four diehards, which is just not enough of a critical mass to get a good exchange going. We limped along for a few more meetings, and then with a shudder gave up the ghost. We had been together for over a decade. We hated to see our group go under. But its death was out of our control.

"These things have a natural life cycle of their own," a friend in another book group remarked when we told him the story of our group's demise. "After a while you know what people will say, you've heard it all before. They just run out of steam." Maybe so. But looking back, we do feel that we could have kept our group on track longer and maintained discussion at a higher level had we known what we were doing. From our interviews and observations around the country, we've gathered that certain problems are endemic to book groups. Recognizing these problems and addressing them head on (and early on) is what this chapter is about.

## Book Discussions Get Derailed

"Our group had been going fine for several years," says Carol, "and then one of the members started having marital problems. No matter what we read, it reminded her of her marriage. It really ruined our discussions. We all felt that she was dragging us through her personal life. Once she got onto it, there was no way to get back to the book."

"I thought if Sally brought up her child once more I would

scream," another group member tells us. "It was as if all world literature revolved around that kid."

"My best friend and I secretly call our group the Toxic Book Club," notes Michelle of her all-women San Francisco group. "Some members feel they have permission to dump whatever they want. They feel safe to say just about anything. These women come out with outrageous personal confessions. I want to talk about books. One woman dropped out, claiming we don't really discuss books. The whole thing is getting too overwhelmed by the personal."

This problem of personal issues intruding on book discussion came up more than any other. Many members complained that one selfish person derailed the conversation or always changed the subject. Other groups suffered from a faction that preferred chitchat and gossip to serious book discussion. Merle says she loved her old north Seattle neighborhood group because it was friendly and cozy, but after a while she wished there was more focus on the books and less on "kids and brownies." From our experience, this tends to be a problem particularly with long-standing, comfortably established groups: members no longer feel the need to impress each other with their intellectual acumen, their lives have been entangled for years, they know all about one another's marriages, children, home improvement projects, jobs, vacations—and they spend more and more time talking about these subjects and less and less on the books. Gradually, the book group becomes indistinguishable from any other social gathering. "It was a lot of fun and we loved seeing one another," remarks one woman whose group succumbed to this problem, "but the books got lost."

We've also heard of groups in which conversation strays into personal issues and gossip because no one knows what to say about the book: "We read *Portrait of the Artist as a Young Man* and the group couldn't even discuss it—they didn't have a clue!" Rebecca complains about her New York City group. "All the members wanted to talk about was their

Catholic parochial schools and how it was sort of like Joyce. Other nights they end up talking about decorating. Or pantyhose—we had a long pantyhose discussion one time. Anyway, on *Portrait of the Artist,* I felt so robbed because I really enjoyed reading it."

Probably the best way to get around this problem is to have someone lead the discussion. Leaders not only throw out ideas and questions to get the ball rolling at the beginning of the meeting, but can tactfully guide the discussion away from the kids, brownies, and pantyhose and back onto James Joyce. A skillful leader can also rescue the group from a domineering bore or a member who keeps dumping his or her personal problems on the others. For more about the role of a leader in book discussion, see Chapter 4.

Even if your group has no formal leader, you as an individual member can be upfront about preserving book discussion time. Take the bull by the horns—interrupt the digression, no matter how rude it feels, and say, "Hey, whoa, hold on a minute—can we get back to the book?" After you've done this a few times, the digressors will at least be aware of what they're doing to the meeting.

Another good way of keeping book discussions on track is to make a formal separation between social time and book time. Lots of groups use the first half hour or so of each meeting for socializing. Then, when it's time to talk about the book, someone will say, "Okay, let's get down to it" and the group shifts gears. Often members move on to a different room—kitchen or den for social time, living room for discussion. This may sound a bit stilted, but the little ceremony helps people focus their attention on the book. It signals that the discussion is a thing apart from "ordinary" life—that it is, in fact, the primary purpose of the meeting.

## Choosing What to Read

Deciding what book to read is a perennial problem, and sometimes an extremely acrimonious one—"a monthly cat fight," as one person put it. Trouble arises most frequently when there is no formal structure for making choices. "It was a free-for-all every month," Deb says of her short-lived New York City group of recent college graduates. "Everyone had ideas, and we would take votes to narrow them down, and then there would be a second round of voting. This took a long time. It was always a stressful part of the evening."

Conrad comments that her group generally devotes half the meeting time to "arguing over what books we're going to read next." In many groups, in fact, the debate over what to read next is always far more heated than the discussion of the book they eventually settle on.

Kristin Kennell strongly advises groups to avoid this problem by making their choices well in advance. We've talked to a couple of groups that use the December meeting for future planning and scheduling. Each person comes prepared with a list of books and the group goes through the calendar for the upcoming year, assigning months and agreeing on which book to read when. There are endless variations on this idea: some groups do the planning twice a year, others plan only three or four months ahead, still others go on a weekend retreat together to plan the meetings. For other suggestions on ways to make book selection run smoothly, see Chapter 3.

Find a method of choosing books that works for your group, but by all means plan ahead in some fashion. If you don't, you'll be floundering around at every meeting, mulling over booklists and getting into arguments. Or, even worse, the books you finally choose will not make for good discussions. This can easily happen if members get so tired of the arguments that they give in and agree to read books they really don't think will work. (Remember, there's a difference between reading a book you dislike and reading a book that just doesn't provide fodder for discussion. Almost everyone we interviewed mentioned to us that there are plenty of good books out there that really aren't "discussable.")

Another common book selection problem arises when one member or a small group of members constantly vetoes other members' book suggestions. We've talked to groups that never choose a book if anyone in the group objects to it—a method that works only because everybody in the group is generally willing to read a variety of things. In other groups, the majority prevails, even if one or two members speak up against a book; usually, the vetoers have the good grace to go ahead and read it—and are often glad they did.

But if your book-choosing sessions frequently get mired down in too many vetoes, you may want to meet the problem head-on. When your naysayer starts in next time, ask frankly how serious this objection is and point out how frequently he or she raises objections to proposed titles. If the problem persists, you may want to suggest that this person find a group more to his or her taste. See "Adding and Subtracting Members" on page 112.

Of course, if a whole faction of the group seems bent on steering book selections in a certain direction, you have a bigger problem. See "Division in the Ranks" on page 108.

If you're just having trouble coming up with acceptable choices, one solution may be to arrange to visit the local bookstore as a group. Some of the bigger and better stores have advisers who meet regularly with book group members and offer presentations of titles. These advisers get to know a particular group's tastes and what has worked for them in the past, and they use this knowledge to work up a list of suggested titles. Some groups make a night of it, bringing wine and cheese or going out for dessert afterward to mull over the books presented. If your local bookstore doesn't offer book group presentations, recommend that they start. "Whenever we go into the Tattered Cover for our presentations, each of us ends up dropping fifty dollars on books we can't resist," one Denverite tells us. That should be incentive enough for any bookseller.

## Division in the Ranks

One woman we interviewed was so inflamed by the interpersonal problems of her book group that she insisted on anonymity. "These women are so narrow-minded, they're so smug," she groans in exasperation. "The group has definitely split into factions—basically it's the rich versus the poor (though, mind you, this is a relative term). It's private versus public school. This is at the root of it. The rich women are ultraprotected and insulated from reality. They are out of touch; they have no personal experience with social reality. Others—a minority—are more socially aware. This breeds resentment and division. It got very bad in the Reagan/Bush years—there were people who were suspected of voting for Bush. One woman calls gay people 'queer.' You can't believe this. Those of us in the other camp get taken aback by these dinosaurs."

Another, and in her mind related, problem concerns the tone of the discussions. "I'm frustrated because the discussions of the books are becoming less and less analytical. These are fully developed brains that are not going any further. People come in without any preparation, without devoting any thought to the book. If they would just prepare a list of questions or themes and stick to that, it would help. I see our discipline melting away." She blames the "dinosaurs" for trivializing the group.

For a while it looked like this group might break up, or that the "poor" faction might split off and start its own group. But for the moment anyway they have decided to stick together. Tensions eased a good deal after the group held a "powwow" at the end of the year at which all the members

could air their grievances. Our contact—let's call her Erica—
was stunned to discover that the dinosaurs were just as pissed
off at *her* as she was at *them*. They complained that she was
sharp-tongued and negative, and several of them felt personally attacked by her. The book group used to be safe and sup-
portive, they claimed, but now the "poor" women were
making it fraught and contentious. One woman was practically reduced to tears, insisting that everyone hated her.

We cringed a bit as Erica described this painful scene, but
she insisted that the powwow actually helped clear the air. If
your group is torn by interpersonal problems, you might try to
arrange something similar. Even relatively amicable groups
find that it's useful to step back every six months or once a
year and talk about how things are going. Are all members
happy with the book choices? Do they feel free to express
their ideas and to disagree with the prevailing opinion? Are
they offended by things that the others have said? Are the tone
and content of the discussions living up to their expectations?
If you can bring problems out in the open early on, you can
keep them from festering.

Rebecca's group of New York City women is still struggling with such problems. "In this group there is a dichotomy
between a faction that just wants to have a good read and discuss it, and a faction that has a real political agenda and wants
to be very current, very politically correct," she explains. (See
if you can tell which faction she counts herself in on.) This
has made both book selection and book discussion a problem, with members sometimes squaring off in two armed
camps. Paradoxically, the group seems to have survived because its other problem—what Rebecca dismisses as some
members' "superficiality" and "lackluster book discussions"—
has blunted the conflict between the two factions. So the
group limps along, held together by the fact that it was
formed of a loose network of friends, as well as by the fact
that they do often pick books that are challenging and worth
reading.

Some divisions, of course, are unavoidable, and even welcome. If everyone agrees all the time, discussions become flat. But when differences of opinion or perspective lead to personal attacks, it's time to talk about it. When the book group ceases to be pleasurable, it has lost one of its primary reasons for being.

## Attendance Problems

A century ago, members of women's study groups were commonly fined for failure to attend. If your group is plagued by attendance problems, you might be tempted to revive this custom. Poor attendance is one of the major reasons why groups disband.

Attendance is such a vital issue that you might even want to raise it at your group's inaugural meeting, when you're setting down the ground rules. As one woman tells us, "When we started out, the question kept coming up: How committed are we? Should we keep doing this? Are we willing to attend each time? At first, our founder kept calling people to ask if they were coming. This helped add cohesiveness and sense of purpose. But now the group is going along on its own steam."

Though it sounds priggish and schoolmarmish, it's probably a good idea to be fairly stern about attendance. When fewer than five people show up, it can be difficult to get a good discussion going. Spotty attendance also creates animosity. Those who do show up feel put-upon, and rightly so: they have canceled other plans, hired a baby-sitter, postponed work, sacrificed precious time with a partner, or made some other change in their routine, only to have other people fail to show—in effect saying, "Who cares?" One long-running group, which has managed successfully to add and subtract several members over the years, considered adopting a hard-nosed "three strikes and you're out" policy: if a member didn't come or didn't finish the book on three consecutive meetings, he or she would be canned.

If poor attendance is becoming a problem in your group, you might want to address the issue head-on at a meeting—or even call a "summit" meeting specifically to try to iron things out. If the problem really stems from some members having too many scheduling conflicts, there are ways to remedy that. For example, you could schedule meetings months or even a year in advance: everyone marks his or her calendar and keeps that day open. Try scheduling the book group for the same day each month—the first Wednesday, the third Monday, or whatever. But if the problem is larger, stemming from a few members beginning to feel alienated and losing interest in the group, then it's best to air the underlying feelings before you lose those members altogether.

In some groups we contacted, the attendance problem was caused simply by a sloppy system of informing members of the meeting times and dates. People who missed one meeting found themselves "out of the loop": nobody told them where or when the next meeting would be, and by the time they contacted another member, the meeting date was already a conflict for them. Denise's Washington, D.C., book club, has a clear system: she sends out a monthly newsletter announcing the upcoming book and telling members where and when the meeting will be held. After someone has missed two meetings in a row, Denise crosses them off the newsletter mailing list: if they want to rejoin for future meetings, it's up to them to reestablish contact. So far, this arrangement has worked out well—but Denise does worry that the group might fall apart if she gives up her caretaking role or tries to pass it on to someone else. She hasn't complained about the time and money involved in circulating a newsletter, but it struck us as inherently unfair for one person to shoulder this task alone. If you want to set up something similar in your book group, try to work out a rotating schedule so that the

job of caretaker passes from member to member every year or
every six months.

## Adding and Subtracting Members

If your group is running out of steam or if attendance is
chronically poor, you may want to consider inviting new
members in. "It's always a good idea to add a new voice,"
says Merrill, a member of a two-year-old group in Chicago.
"After a while you get to know what everyone is going to say.
Discussions get predictable. We added a new member recently and it has really livened things up." We managed to
squeeze a couple more years out of our old New York group
when we asked Paula and Arthur to join—both were enthusiastic readers who always finished the book, and were not at
all shy about voicing their opinions.

But you do need to exercise some caution before you embark on an expansion program. Group members should first
agree on how many new members they want (remember that
an optimal size is about ten to twelve) and decide on some
method for recruiting them. Ellen says her group got out of
hand when some members began bringing along friends
whenever they felt like it and without clearing it first with the
others: on some evenings the group was crowded with strangers who were more interested in hanging out and meeting
new people than in talking about books. This created a lot of
tension and animosity.

Once a group has been meeting for a while, you'll have a
clear sense of what kind of people will feel comfortable in it.
Rather than invite total strangers to join, you'll probably want
to ask someone who's a friend of one of the current
members—not necessarily a close friend, but at least someone
whom the current member can vouch for.

We sat in on a Seattle book group that had advertised for

new members through a bookstore bulletin board. One woman—let's call her Karen—had been interviewed by phone and seemed fine, but when the evening came for her to attend, Karen totally dominated the group, grilled each member about his or her career, drank too much wine, and droned on and on about her personal life. The group was stunned and embarrassed—and someone was assigned the unpleasant task of uninviting her. That person decided to brush Karen off gently by telling her that the group members felt that they had enough members after all. Karen put up a struggle, apologized for her behavior, and promised it wouldn't happen again. So the group's representative had to get tougher and say bluntly, "We just didn't think that you'd fit in." And that was that. The moral is: proceed slowly and with due deliberation.

Getting rid of unwanted group members is usually a lot more difficult than finding new ones. Denise recalls that a woman who once began to attend her Washington, D.C., group seemed determined *not* to discuss the book they had chosen. "She had a Ph.D. and she only wanted to talk about all the other books she'd read," Denise says. "We kind of let her know that we were here to talk about this book. She never came back—I guess she figured out herself that she didn't fit in."

This technique—let's call it The Big Chill—has worked for a number of groups we talked to, which really surprised us. Knowing how obtuse some people can be, we were impressed to hear how often these misfits sensed that the other group members didn't like them and just stopped coming, all on their own.

But if you're saddled with a terrible bore, or a drunk, or a person who won't let anyone else speak, or a pugnacious brat, or groupwrecker of some other stripe who simply won't take the hint that he/she is unwelcome, you may have to resort to blunter tactics. This is one case where having a paid presenter offers unexpected benefits: In Ginny's group in

Washington, D.C., the hired leader Helen spoke to one obnoxious member and told her to stop coming to the group's meetings since she never finished the book anyway. Judy's Cambridge, Massachusetts, group faced a similar situation: "David's girlfriend started coming for a while, but she was very intense—too intense. We were more laid back. She compiled a list of all the books we'd read and wanted us to sit down one night and rate the books we'd read already. She wanted to keep the list on her computer. We told her to get lost." By all means do the same when necessary. Reading group time is too precious to let it be spoiled just because everyone in your group is too shy or too polite to boot out a boor.

## Failure to Finish the Book

"Some people never finish or even bother to read the books," Stephanie complains of her long-running Denver group. "They are the same people each time. They look at the group as a social get-together club."

When too many members fail to finish the book, it's obviously impossible to carry on an intelligent conversation about it. Rebecca noted with horror that eight out of the ten women in her club didn't read *Anna Karenina,* but came to the meeting anyway (a couple of them actually read the Cliff Notes instead). One woman was so disgusted by this that she quit the club.

But problems also arise when only one or two people don't make it to the end. They beg the others not to reveal the ending or they continually interrupt the discussion with questions that would have been obvious if they had finished. Conversation becomes stilted, tempers flare, and the majority who did finish feel cheated out of a good evening of discourse.

Even more friction arises when some members *deliberately*

choose not to finish the book. In some groups—like David's group in Indianapolis—not finishing a book is regarded as a legitimate comment on that book, and rather than apologize, the nonfinishers are loud and vocal about *why* the book didn't grab their interest. But most groups expect more of an effort. "I felt personally attacked when some of the other people in my group refused to finish Cormac McCarthy's *Blood Meridian*," said Arthur of his couples group in Portland, Oregon. "They read three chapters and said it was gross and wouldn't go on. This really annoyed me."

You obviously can't force people to complete the reading, and if you get too pissy about it you'll spoil the tone of the group, making it seem too much like school. But it does make sense to set down certain rules. Make it clear that you're not going to hold up discussion or keep the ending a secret for those who didn't get through the whole book. Agree that all should make a good-faith attempt to finish the book even if they hate it. After all, some of the best discussions arise when members disagree violently on a book's merits. But you can't debate fairly or cogently if some people have only read the first couple of chapters.

If your group has one or two members who just never seem to read the whole book, you may want to boot them out. Alternatively, they may be such lively, charming people that you decide to tolerate their slackness. But if several members aren't finishing the books on a regular basis, it could be that your book choices are at fault. Your group might want to choose different kinds of books—shorter ones or more accessible ones, or books that are so gripping no one can bear to put them down. Book clubs do get into ruts: too many classics, too many novels by contemporary women, too many books about gender issues. Shake yourselves up by radically shifting gears now and then. Give yourselves a month or two off. If you've chosen a really long book that few members have finished, discuss the first half at one meeting and then schedule a second meeting to wrap things up.

## Special Events

If your book group is getting stale and needs a shot of energy, consider staging some sort of special event. Here are some ideas gleaned from the groups we've contacted, visited, or participated in:

- See (or rent) the movie version of a book you have read together. Movies based on great novels abound—from *Madame Bovary* to *The Remains of the Day,* from *Moby-Dick* to *The Bonfire of the Vanities.* Some are faithful to the books, others are their own work of art—which in itself opens a rich vein of discussion. But do make sure you see the film together. Otherwise, members who didn't see it may resent having book discussion dominated by references to the movie version.

- Go to a lecture or reading together. Contemporary authors are constantly hitting the road to promote their books. Coordinate your book group with an appearance by the author. No matter how well you think you know a writer's work, it's always surprising to see the creator in the flesh.

- Turn one evening into a night for reading aloud. Read a one-act play out loud together and talk about it or arrange for each member to bring in a few favorite poems to read aloud and discuss. One group we interviewed, for instance, reads a Shakespeare play aloud every April to celebrate the Bard's birthday. We've even heard of a group holding an Erotic Evening, with each member reading aloud passages from her favorite erotic book (all the refreshments that night were chocolate and sinfully rich).

- If you're in a single-sex group, invite spouses, partners, or friends of the opposite sex along to a meeting. Ask them to read the book too—but make sure it's a selection that is not too provocative or controversial.

- Visit a library together and have a librarian take the group on a tour. Ginny's group in Washington, D.C., toured the Library of Congress (since one of the members is married to the head of the library, we suspect they got special treatment). You'll be amazed at the new resources that even small local libraries now have, thanks to the computer revolution. Knowing your way around a library can be a big help in doing research for a presentation.

- Invite a guest lecturer or author. Have a scholar from a local college come to chat with the group about a book that falls within his/her area of expertise. Riskier, but maybe worth trying, is to invite the author of the book to the group. Sue Miller got a ton of publicity when she visited book groups as part of her promotional tour for *For Love.* "It worked out very well, though we had our reservations about it," comments Stephanie, whose Denver group was one of the ones Miller visited. "We tried to carry on an honest discussion as if she weren't there, although we did direct a lot of questions to her. Of course we were all curious about how autobiographical her books are. Luckily, most of us really like her books."

- Plan an activity that ties in with the book you're reading. One group went line dancing after they read *Cowboys Are My Weakness* by Pam Houston. Another group read Carol Pearson's *The Hero Within,* which describes six basic archetypes people live by. Instead of having their usual discussion, they broke into small groups and worked out which archetype applied to each member. Larry's group went to a ballgame together after reading George Will's *Men at Work.* Brad's group read *Alice in*

*Wonderland* for Halloween and had each member come dressed as a character from the book.

- Hold a book group retreat. Go away for a weekend together or spend a day hiking, biking, or picnicking. It's even more fun if you can tie it in with your book—for example, a book about natural history or regional history or gardening.

## When to Cut Your Losses

"I knew a guy who had been in the same book club for twenty-five years," a San Francisco friend reports, "and finally one day he said: 'I know what everyone is going to say, I never want to hear them say it again,' And that was it. He just stopped going."

When the group becomes a chore or a bore, it's time to call it quits. Resign. Let your group die gracefully. Steal away the members you like best and start your own splinter group. Find a new group to join on your own. Let the old group go dormant for a while and see if anyone else wants to revive it.

It's funny, when our old group finally bit the dust, we were sorry to see it go, but also just a little bit relieved. With no book group, we had more free time to read what we *really* wanted. We didn't have to crank ourselves up anymore for the monthly meeting, arming ourselves beforehand for the arguments we could all too well predict. We could browse in a bookstore without feeling compelled to hunt for the perfect title, only to have the others groan at the idea of plowing through *that* dreadful book. We could spend that extra night out each month doing whatever we felt like doing—one less commitment, one less obligation.

But then, within a few months, Holly found a new group and David, after moving across the country, organized his own. Without a book group, you see, something was missing from our lives.

It wasn't that we'd lost touch with the group members, for some of them had become close friends whom we continued to see. And of course both of us had kept reading whenever we could.

What was missing was the combination of books and people—a mix that one gets only in a book group. We both found, to our surprise, that this combination was something we did not want to be without.

Lucky for us, we live in a time when lots and lots of other people feel the same way.

# 7

# The Book Lists

In all our interviews with reading group members around the country, the one question that never failed to get people talking was, "What books have you read?" We found ourselves eagerly trading titles with people, each of us scribbling down the names and tucking them away in special places so we could propose those books at the next meeting of our own groups. The better-organized people whipped out their groups' ongoing book list, making quick verbal annotations—"We really fought over that one."; "I hated it at the time, but now I actually think it was good."; "This one just blew us away."; "Don't even THINK about reading this one!"

Members of book clubs are inveterate seekers-out of good books to read, specifically of good *discussable* books to read (as people told us time and again, there are plenty of good books that don't generate enough discussion to last ten minutes). Here, then, is our gift to you: an annotated list of book titles that have thrilled, infuriated, and somehow stirred up various reading groups we know. We've tried to steer you toward books that will match the particular tastes of your group, whatever those may be. Of course, you can still spend those hours browsing through bookstores for your own discoveries—we wouldn't rob you of one of life's choicer pleasures. But at those end-of-meeting free-for-alls when you're picking your next book to read, we trust this section of our book will come in very handy.

## Top Ten Book Club Hits

**Palace Walk** by Naguib Mahfouz (498 pp.) It's unlike anything else you've ever read—a long, slow-moving mesmerizing portrait of an Egyptian merchant's family. Despite the rather stiff prose style (translated from the Egyptian), you'll read on to learn about this culture—and end up caring more deeply than you imagine about these irritating individuals. Many readers go into a meeting convinced they didn't like this book, but after hours of animated discussion realize they loved it.

**The Remains of the Day** by Kazuo Ishiguro (245 pp.) Narrated by the quintessential English butler, this novel depicts the upstairs-downstairs world of a country house. Below the polished surface, however, it's a complicated, ambivalent look at a society on its last legs. The theme is essentially what it means to be British—curious, considering the author's Japanese heritage. Or maybe it's not so curious . . .

**The Age of Innocence** by Edith Wharton (various editions; Penguin edition, 301 pp.) In this tale of Newland Archer's hopeless love for Countess Ellen Olenska, Wharton creates her sharpest social commentary on the manners and taboos of "Old New York." Yet to read this as a costume drama is to miss the complexity of Wharton's attitude toward New York, a city she despised and fled, yet belonged to irrevocably. Her memoirs, *A Backward Glance,* shed much light here.

*A **Thousand Acres*** by Jane Smiley (371 pp.) With consider-able passion and ingenuity, Smiley transplants Shakespeare's *King Lear* to a contemporary Iowa farm—with Ginny (Gon-eril) narrating the devastating crack-up of her abusive father Larry Cook (the Lear figure). This concept may strike some as overly schematic, and yet Smiley plays so powerfully off our sympathies and expectations that discussion is bound to be lively.

***Beloved*** by Toni Morrison (275 pp.) Set in rural Ohio in the first postslavery generation, this richly peopled novel centers on Sethe, who is accompanied throughout her life by Be-loved, the spirit of her long-ago dead child. As always, Morrison focuses on how African-Americans try to forge a life of dignity, sorting out family and sex and spiritual belief. But did she need the ghost device here? Opinions may be sharply divided.

***Love in the Time of Cholera*** by Gabriel García Marquez (348 pp.) Book groups rave over this rich novel by the Nobel Prize-winning Colombian. It's a lyrical story of a middle-aged triangle of lovers, told in an elegantly poised writing style. Some readers never get used to García Marquez's "magical realism"—fantastic details that heighten the symbolism—while others eat it up; this is one book where discussion of tech-nique gets impassioned.

***Madame Bovary*** by Gustave Flaubert (various editions; Pen-guin edition 292 pp.) Many of you have already read this masterpiece about the wretched marriage and disastrous af-fairs of a provincial French woman. But rereading will allow you to delve deeper into such questions as: Why did Flaubert lavish so much art on so foolish a heroine? Can a man really imagine himself to *be* a woman, as Flaubert claimed he could? And is this in some sense a novel about the evils of reading fiction?

**The Handmaid's Tale** by Margaret Atwood (395 pp.) Less science fiction than it is future-shock fable, Atwood's novel delineates a society where women greatly outnumber men, and thus are each assigned to narrow roles—childbearer *or* sexual object *or* mistress of the household—while men live full, powerful lives. While it seems remote from our own society, you may be surprised in discussion to see how passionately, even furiously, people react.

**Angle of Repose** by Wallace Stegner (569 pp.) Book clubs love Wallace Stegner, and this is his blockbuster, a big sprawling novel about a curmudgeonly retired California historian uncovering the story of his grandparents' emigration westward, while he himself copes with the dislocation of the sixties. Jam-packed with politics, American social history, relations between the sexes and between the generations, it's written in taut, luminously intelligent prose.

**The Road to Coorain** by Jill Ker Conway (238 pp.) In a lucid, unsentimental writing style, Conway recounts her childhood on a remote Australian sheep farm—particularly her mother's stubborn fight to keep the farm going after Jill's dad dies. Tough frontier living seen up close, with a marvelous female heroine.

## Books to Revel In

**A Bend in the River** by V. S. Naipaul (278 pp.) The narrator of this searing novel is an Indian trader who takes over a shabby shop on the market square of a remote African town. Salim, a Moslem, comes to Africa to escape his narrow past—but he finds himself caught in a world of inexplicable violence, racial hatreds, and absolute solitude. Naipaul, a Hindu born in Trinidad, carries on the great tradition of Conrad and Graham Greene.

**Animal Dreams** by Barbara Kingsolver (342 pp.) Even though this novel sounds like a litany of politically correct elements—Native American culture, the landscape of the American Southwest, the war in Nicaragua, the corporate pollution threatening small farmers, the redemptive love between women—the story is so moving and so powerfully told that you forgive Kingsolver just about anything. Plenty of issues and vivid characters to discuss.

**The Makioka Sisters** by Junichiro Tanizaki (538 pp.) The sisters of Tanizaki's proper Kyoto family find themselves impaled on Japan's abrupt postwar modernization, and each responds in a totally different way. This book is as fascinating for its superb artistry as for its insights into the Japanese psyche and sexual mores.

**Portrait of a Lady** by Henry James (various editions; Modern Library edition, 591 pp.) James's early triumph has his creepiest villain (Gilbert Osmond), his most seductively complicated villainess (Serena Merle), and his most controversial heroine—your group is bound to split into factions that either adore or abhor Isabel Archer. That final kiss brings up the vexed (but ever fascinating) question of James's sexuality.

**The Collected Stories of Katherine Anne Porter** by Katherine Anne Porter (459 pp.) It's too bad Porter is remembered nowadays chiefly for the sprawling *Ship of Fools,* for her true gift was to compress an entire world into about fifty pages. "Noon Wine," her masterpiece, a tale of possibly justified homicide on a shabby Texas farm, has the stark moral urgency of a Greek tragedy; "Old Mortality" and "The Old Order" expose the trumped-up romance of the Old South.

**Dubliners** by James Joyce (various editions; Penguin edition, 223 pp.) Joyce's stories of Dublin's tired and poor are quiet, understated, bleak, and heaving with suppressed fury. It's one of those books that are too often read only in college (or worse, high school); now that you're grown, what do you make of Gabriel's solitary anguish at the end of "The Dead"?

**I, Claudius** by Robert Graves (432 pp.) Masterpiece Theater turned this and *Claudius the God* into a soap opera in Roman drag, but the books are even more delicious than the television series (which you can rent on video). A good jumping-off point would be to place the Claudius books in the context of Graves's very strange life, which included a stint on the front in World War I, two fraught marriages, and lots of now-neglected verse.

**The Reef** by Edith Wharton (356 pp.) Everyone reads *The Age of Innocence* and *The House of Mirth,* but *The Reef* is oddly compelling, revealing Wharton's sexual fantasies and her fear of being "the woman to whom nothing ever happened." Wharton's friend Henry James especially admired this story of a love triangle, played out by three Americans at a French chateau. It's ripe for Masterpiece Theater—casting ideas, anyone?

**Bonfire of the Vanities** by Tom Wolfe (690 pp.) A thick, immensely satisfying book that does for 1980s New York City what Dickens's novels did for nineteenth-century London—the one difference being that Wolfe's broad cast of social types doesn't include a single really likeable character. But the complicated plot hangs together like a dream, and the satire is bitingly on target.

**The Great Gatsby** by F. Scott Fitzgerald (189 pp.) Another of those classics we all read too early, *Gatsby* definitely rewards rereading. It's the poignant love story of Jay Gatsby, self-made millionaire, and Daisy Buchanan, wife of a polo-playing neighbor on Long Island's ritzy North Shore. It's also a commentary on the American dream, just as apt for the 1990s as for the 1920s. Fitzgerald's prose style is graceful, poised, and passionate—they just don't write 'em like this anymore.

## Sure to Provoke Debate

*Lolita* by Vladimir Nabokov (288 pp.) Classic status has not dimmed the sheer weirdness of Nabokov's best-known and most controversial book. Underneath its high literary gloss, cartoon-bright snapshots of America in the 1950s, allusions to Edgar Allan Poe, and nostalgia for Europe, this is still, shockingly, the confessions of a child molester. You can probably spend your entire meeting discussing *why* Nabokov wrote this novel.

*Will You Please Be Quiet, Please?* by Raymond Carver (249 pp.) You're either going to love or loathe these spare, laconic stories about marginal, depressed, depressing characters—a salesman between jobs, a postman who tries to piece together an odd couple's life, a neurotic Native American out in the boondocks of Washington State. Carver's fans rave about his use of language and his brooding sense of imminent revelation; his critics insist he has all the faults of Ann Beattie and none of her virtues.

*A Good Scent From a Strange Mountain* by Robert Olen Butler (249 pp.) In this Pulitzer Prize-winning collection of stories, a hitherto little-known American writer gives voices to members of the expatriate Vietnamese community living in Lake Charles, Louisiana. Olen's fourteen narrators—bargirls and waitresses, small businessmen and jealous husbands—all thrive, however modestly, in America; but each has fallen victim to our soft, soulless culture. Olen makes us see our own souls through their eyes.

***The Executioner's Song*** by Norman Mailer (1,024 pp.) This monster is mostly spliced transcripts of tapes detailing the life and times of deranged Utah murderer Gary Gilmore. Did the ever-controversial Mailer lose his mind? Or is this some kind of weird late twentieth-century epic, a bizarre cross-pollination between Homer and Truman Capote? And is Gilmore the hero or the villain?

***Blood Meridian*** by Cormac McCarthy (337 pp.) We've heard of groups that nearly came to blows over this gruesome saga of the West, which McCarthy wrote several years before he hit it big with *All the Pretty Horses.* Blood saturates these adventures of a bunch of American mercenaries hired to kill every Indian they come across. The writing is reminiscent of Faulkner and Melville—but can any amount of art excuse so much carnage?

***Outerbridge Reach*** by Robert Stone (409 pp.) The most likely inheritor of Hemingway's mantle as the macho king, Stone is a gifted writer who writes about men doing unabashedly manly things—in this case, competing in a long-distance sailing race. Along the way, of course, lots of stuff about sex, survival, and courage, expounded by a complexly masculine protagonist. The genders may well divide in their assessment.

***Dreaming in Cuban*** by Cristina García (245 pp.) Lots to talk about here—the place of women in Latin American families, Cuban-American relations, how politics divide families and generations, and the Afro-Cuban practice of *santería,* which plays an important role in this novel. Reviewers compared this book to Gabriel García Marquez, Isabel Allende, even Chekhov. Does it deserve such high praise?

***Continental Drift*** by Russell Banks (421 pp.) Powerful and upsetting, Russell Banks's "breakthrough" novel is sure to electrify your group. Bob Dubois is a kind of contemporary everyman who leaves his dead-end life in depressed New Hampshire to find comfort and happiness in Florida. Instead he finds drugs, illegal aliens, corruption, desperation, and voodoo. Banks floats enough "issues" to fill a thousand op-ed pages: the question is, does he really integrate them into the novel?

***The Secret History*** by Donna Tartt (503 pp.) We were prepared to hate this over-hyped "voice of a generation" novel, but from page one we loved it. A treacherous clique of effete students at a small New England college sucks an innocent newcomer into their web of snobbery, dissipation, malice, and ultimately murder. Intelligent, literate writing is wed to a page-turner plot. Everyone will want to argue about these detestable characters.

## Unforgettable Individuals

***The Horse's Mouth*** by Joyce Cary (345 pp.) Gulley Jimson, gifted painter, freeloader, and carouser, is one of the most memorable characters of English fiction. Seeing 1940s London through his eyes is a surrealistic visual show indeed, and throughout this picaresque novel Jimson reels off his iconoclastic meditations on art, society, and morals in a spirited, colloquial voice. A very funny, invigorating, exhilarating book.

***All the King's Men*** by Robert Penn Warren (438 pp.) This Pulitzer Prize-winner, now a neglected classic, is still one of the most astute political novels to come out of America. There's something almost Roman in the way the theme of "power corrupts" is dramatized in the career of a Deep South politician, based on Huey Long. The literary allusions planted within the tough-talking first-person narrative will really test your cultural literacy.

***The Screwtape Letters*** by C. S. Lewis (172 pp.) The correspondence of veteran devil Screwtape to his young nephew Wormwood, just starting out in the business of corrupting human souls, is a shrewdly funny and yet very serious examination of the nature of evil. A Cambridge professor and devout Christian, Lewis wrote with wit, intelligence, and great psychological insight; it's a refreshing argument for thinking people of any religion.

***Fifth Business*** by Robertson Davies (266 pp.) A childhood accident forever ties together three boys: Davies's Deptford trilogy devotes one book to each boy's life. This is the first and the best. Though its hero, schoolmaster and historian Dunstan Ramsay, is the least flamboyant of the three, he regales us with the lives of the other two—a master magician and a scoundrel tycoon—in an intelligent, urbane voice. A full-blooded book, satisfying in an old-fashioned way.

***Under the Volcano*** by Malcolm Lowry (375 pp.) A day in the drunken life of Geoffrey Firmin, British consul in provincial Mexico. The gifted, self-destructive consul both repels and gains our sympathy; his long day's journey into night is a harrowing examination of wasted talent, frustrated love, and bitter abandon. Does his wife cheat on him because he drinks, or does he drink because she cheats? In a portrait this complex, there are no easy answers.

***Ironweed*** by William P. Kennedy (240 pp.) This Pulitzer Prize-winning novel follows Francis Phelan into the depths of homelessness and alcoholism, proving that even a bum can be a man to reckon with. He's a raggedy figure who's been a failure at everything—baseball, fatherhood, marriage, son-hood—but his intelligence and remorse give him surprising dignity. For a broader (and in some ways more powerful) canvas of Kennedy's Albany, read *Billy Phelan's Greatest Game,* about Francis's son.

**Celestial Navigation** by Anne Tyler (249 pp.) Many members of your group may have read Tyler's later best-sellers, but you'll be pleasantly surprised by this earlier novel, the story of Jeremy, a thirty-eight-year-old bachelor who has never left home. Is he an eccentric, a simpleton, a neglected artistic genius? Drawn into his narrow, rich world, we learn about love and the gift of letting people be themselves.

**Midnight's Children** by Salman Rushdie (522 pp.) Before Rushdie became the target of Islamic fundamentalists for his novel *The Satanic Verses,* he was known primarily for this sprawling novel/allegory/hallucination about the birth pangs of contemporary India, narrated by the wonderfully grotesque Saleem Sinai. Like Gabriel García Marquez, Rushdie flips effortlessly back and forth between fantasy and history. This novel is a total immersion in India: past, present, and mythological.

## The Marriage Knot

**Anna Karenina** by Leo Tolstoy (various editions; Penguin edition, 853 pp.) This vast, powerful novel of Imperial Russia centers on the doomed adultery of Anna, wife of coldly brilliant politician Karenin, and handsome young officer Count Vronsky. Tolstoy surrounds his tragic lovers with a complex web of personalities and events—you'll ache for the characters, they seem so real. This is definitely a book for grown-ups; discussion will lead you deeper into its unrelenting inspection of life's realities.

***The Awakening*** by Kate Chopin (153 pp.) A New Orleans woman who "has it all"—marriage, two children, social position—still isn't satisfied; she's ripe for the kind of adulterous affair that blows everyone to bits. Readers weren't ready for this book when it first appeared in 1899, and Chopin, discouraged, basically quit writing. But now that it has finally come into its own, it's a perennial favorite with women's groups.

***Mrs. Bridge*** by Evan S. Connell (246 pp.) Kansas City country-club matron India Bridge is a perfect specimen of a vanished type—prewar Wasp society hostess—and Connell uses the minutiae of her repressed, circumscribed life to draw a touching portrait of what it means to be a wife, mother, lover, homemaker, and woman. The companion book, *Mr. Bridge,* does the same for her lawyer husband, giving us the male side of the coin.

***Portrait of a Marriage*** by Nigel Nicolson (257 pp.) Homosexual English diplomat Harold Nicolson was married to Vita Sackville-West, a poet and novelist better known today as Virginia Woolf's lover and as the creator of the great gardens at Sissinghurst Castle. Written by their son, this is a tribute to this unusual Edwardian couple's affectionate, broadminded, and enduring partnership.

***Rabbit, Run*** by John Updike (249 pp.) Harry "Rabbit" Angstrom is a high-school basketball star gone to seed, selling used cars in a dreary small Pennsylvania town. Caught between an alcoholic wife, a strident mistress, and his own soured dreams, Rabbit struggles inarticulately to find himself. Rabbit ages (ungracefully) in three sequels—choose the one that matches your group's stage of life. Updike's prose is a thing of beauty and a joy forever.

**Mrs. Caliban** by Rachel Ingalls (125 pp.) A bored California housewife falls adulterously in love with a hulking green man from the sea, escaped from a scientific laboratory. The American-born writer has lived in England too long to pull off the social comedy, but on the metaphoric level it's an insightful study of how marriages go sour and what women really want.

**Come to Me** by Amy Bloom (175 pp.) A young woman tries to understand the love triangle between her mother, her father, and her father's best friend. Another sadder but wiser woman starkly recounts how her beloved older sister lost her mind and then her life. The white widow of a black musician consoles her stepson with sex. In her first collection of stories, psychoanalyst Amy Bloom does not shy away from Big Subjects, but her voice is so strong, and her characters so carefully drawn, that she pulls it off.

## Parents and Children

**Sons and Lovers** by D. H. Lawrence (420 pp.) Paul Morel's struggle to become a man is complicated by his strong-willed mother, a dissatisfied coal miner's wife who lives through her children. This autobiographical novel vividly evokes northern industrial prewar England, the writing style is free of Lawrence's later clichés, and the family dynamics are so powerfully felt that group members may well bare their souls in response.

**To the Lighthouse** by Virginia Woolf (310 pp.) The literary cottage industry spawned by Woolf's life too often makes us lose sight of her art. This is her best novel, drawn from memories of seaside holidays with her impossibly brilliant, complicated family; it fairly seethes with the secret, pent-up passions of childhood. Bloomsbury devotees will recognize every character as a player in Woolf's real-life drama.

***A Death in the Family*** by James Agee (318 pp.) Tragedy strikes a middle-class family in Knoxville, Tennessee, circa 1915, when Jay Follett is killed in a late-night car wreck. Agee's delicate, evocative prose brings to life the whole family—parents, grandparents, cousins, uncles, and aunts—centered on young Rufus Follett, his life forever altered. A period piece or a timeless universal drama? Either way, in the end it's gloriously life-affirming.

***The Man Who Loved Children*** by Christina Stead (504 pp.) This big, sprawling novel is also curiously claustrophic, as it sucks the reader into the ramshackle household of Sam and Henny Pollitt. Like two opposing forces of life, Sam and Henny try to destroy each other through their huge brood of children. Anyone who's ever been a parent or a child will empathize—but with which one of the protagonists? That's where your discussion starts.

***The Good Mother*** by Sue Miller (310 pp.) Recently divorced Anna has one thing going for her—an adoring relationship with her four-year-old daughter. But just as Anna begins to rediscover herself as an independent woman, her ex-husband launches a bitter custody battle, calling into question the one thing she always prided herself on. This disturbing novel makes its readers draw passionate battle lines—not just between women and men but between women and women as well.

***Fortunate Lives*** by Robb Forman Dew (285 pp.) As they prepare for their oldest son to go off to his freshman year at Harvard, an upper-middle-class family faces anew its unhealed—and unhealable—grief over the death of another son. Dew has a deft gift for laying out in detail all the mechanisms and nuances of family life. Compare to Judith Guest's *Ordinary People,* also about the aftermath of a child's death.

**Prince of Tides** by Pat Conroy (664 pp.) Though it's cast in the best-seller mold—obligatory sex and mental breakdowns, layered flashbacks that finally reveal a scandalous family secret—this novel of a family in South Carolina low country is undeniably powerful. The complicated plot will generate discussion, and the characters are complex enough to sharply divide opinion. The protagonist is male, but it's not at all a "guy book"—a good choice for co-ed groups.

**Anywhere But Here** by Mona Simpson (535 pp.) Teenaged Ann August and her divorced mother Adele leave a dreary midwestern factory town and hit the road for California, hoping to launch Ann's movie career. Jumping forward and backward in time, the novel takes us to the heart of their entangled, abusive relationship. An ugly look at American rootlessness—sure to provoke both literary discussion and personal reflections.

**This Boy's Life** by Tobias Wolff (288 pp.) A clear-eyed memoir of a 1950s boyhood, with a twist: Toby's vivacious divorced mom takes her son west to find their fortune, only to burden him with an abusive stepfather. Read in conjunction with *The Duke of Deception,* brother Geoffrey Wolff's biography of their real father (whom Geoffrey had stayed with after the divorce)—this woman sure had a talent for picking wrong men.

**Before and After** by Rosellen Brown (354 pp.) This is a true crime novel in the tradition of Truman Capote's *In Cold Blood*—but much more horrifying because both the victim and the killer are kids in a small New Hampshire town. Poet and novelist Brown creates incredible suspense, asking not just who did it (we learn this in the first pages) but the more disturbing questions of *how* and *why*. It may be the ultimate dysfunctional family book.

***Monkeys*** by Susan Minot (159 pp.) Nine vignettes carry the Vincent family—all seven children—through thirteen years of childhood, adolesence, and coming of age. Rarely has a novelist captured so well the interplay between kids in a large family; each personality is distinct, but shifting alliances, petty squabbles, and shared moments of crisis and laughter bind them into a whole. Touching and utterly believable.

## From a Child's Perspective

***Huckleberry Finn*** by Mark Twain (various editions; Penguin edition, 336 pp.) Young vagabond Huck rafts down the Mississippi River with escaped slave Jim, embarking on the greatest journey in American literature. Get past the Missouri dialect and the nineteenth-century racial standards, and you've got a deeply human, wise, coming-of-age novel, seen through the eyes of a true innocent. Don't forget to read passages aloud— Twain is still the funniest writer *ever*. Period.

***What Maisie Knew*** by Henry James (various editions; Penguin edition, 275 pp.) Maisie is such a child as only Henry James could have invented—wise, wide-eyed, forgiving, alert to nuance, and clinging to her last shreds of innocence as she observes her divorced parents pursue their glamorous, rivalrous, ultimately vicious lives in London. It helps to remember that James himself was obsessed—and perplexed—by adult sexuality, so the real question here is what Henry knew.

***Death of the Heart*** by Elizabeth Bowen (317 pp.) Anna and Thomas Quayne's London household is disrupted by the arrival of Portia, Thomas's sixteen-year-old half-sister, whose irregular childhood on the continent has left her curiously unsuited for life with these sophisticated young marrieds. In elegant, tightly controlled prose, Bowen guides us through a treacherous world where nothing is said, all implied.

***To Kill a Mockingbird*** by Harper Lee (284 pp.) This 1961 Pulitzer prize winner shows a small Alabama town pulled apart by the trial of a black man, accused of raping a white woman. Narrated by the defense counsel's tomboy daughter, this is also a novel about growing up, about tolerance, and about moral courage. Lee's lyrical prose style, superb ear for southern dialect, and perfect memory of childhood make it deeply affecting.

***The Catcher in the Rye*** by J. D. Salinger (214 pp.) Sixteen-year-old Holden Caulfield goes AWOL from boarding school, spending a dissolute couple of days on his own in New York City. Even if you read it as a teenager, you'll see much more in it now, and it may stir up reminiscences from everyone in your group. Two questions to ponder: Why do school libraries ban this book? And why did it make Salinger so famous that he turned into a recluse?

***Floating in My Mother's Palm*** by Ursula Hegi (187 pp.) This quiet gem is about a girl, Hanna Malter, growing up in a small German town in the decade after World War II. It's really a series of sketches—there's one about the gossiping dwarf librarian, one about swimming with her mother, one about the odd young male boarder who is black and blue each week after his "friend" visits, one about her baby brother's death. Haunting and heartbreaking.

## Gender Issues

*Finding Our Fathers* by Samuel Osherson (253 pp.) Published at the outset of the men's movement, this respected book foregoes mythology and drum beating to focus on men's unfinished business with their fathers. The central idea is that men carry around inside them a sense of their fathers as rejecting, incompetent, or absent; some readers find this a seminal idea, while others laugh it off. But it's sure to provoke a lively exchange, no matter what the gender composition of your group.

*A Room of One's Own* by Virginia Woolf (114 pp.) What should one call this spellbinding masterpiece of feminist rhetoric—an essay? A tirade? A dramatic monologue? Woolf's thesis is simple—women must have money and privacy if they want to write—but her method of argument takes in the Brontës, Jane Austen, Aphra Behn, and Shakespeare's imaginary sister. It is even more magnificent (and funny!) read aloud.

*In a Different Voice* by Carol Gilligan (177 pp.) The book that launched a thousand debates about the way men and women view relationships, morality, and values. Are women more "caring" and "relational" than men? Do women and men hold fundamentally different concepts of justice? Is this book an insidious attack on feminism's achievements? Or does it finally acknowledge the female voice that has been ignored too long? Your group will no doubt launch into its own debate.

*Women Who Run with the Wolves* by Clarissa Pinkola Estes (520 pp.) The author of this surprise best-seller is a Jungian analyst and a storyteller who urges women to reconnect with the "wild woman" within. What exactly is this wild woman? The female soul? The rich, instinctive sensuality that society crushes out of little girls? The life/death/life force? Each of the mythic stories that Estes so powerfully tells adds a new facet to this shimmering symbol.

**Conundrum** by Jan Morris (176 pp.) In this deeply moving book, Morris describes what it was like to grow up a woman trapped inside a man's body and how she decided to undergo a sex change operation. As James Morris, the author married, fathered five children, and launched a successful writing career; as Jan Morris, she at last found fulfillment (and she still could write!). Fascinating reflections on the nature of masculinity and femininity.

**Composing a Life** by Mary Catherine Bateson (241 pp.) Bateson examines her own life and that of four friends, all well-educated professionals. As each chapter probes a specific issue and how each of the five dealt with it, a book-long tapestry is woven of trade-offs, triumphs, and redefined priorities. While women's groups will probably use this as a springboard for sharing anecdotes, mixed groups may argue over why the process is different for men and women.

**Between Women: Love, Envy, and Competition in Women's Friendships** by Luise Eichenbaum and Susie Orbach (223 pp.) This study of the complex, contradictory relationships between women may produce an explosive meeting, especially if you're in an all-women group. What is special about the deep friendships between women? And why are these friendships so often rocked by anger, envy, and a sense of betrayal? The authors (best friends and colleagues) answer these questions with lots of examples.

**Fire in the Belly** by Sam Keen (272 pp.) Along with Robert Bly's *Iron John,* this was one of the seminal books of the so-called men's movement. The theme here is that, to achieve true manhood, men must take a spiritual journey, working through alienation and self-imprisonment to achieve a vision of themselves as men with "fire in the belly and passion in [the] heart." The women in your group may wonder if men really relate to this stuff; men may be surprised to find how much they do relate.

## Gay and Lesbian Voices

***Becoming a Man*** by Paul Monette (278 pp.) This memoir of growing up gay in the fifties and sixties won the National Book Award in 1992—probably as much for the stark candor of the voice as for the quality of writing. Monette's coming to terms with his sexuality was full of pain, panic, and self-loathing; even a sexless life seemed preferable at many junctures for him. By avoiding the cliches of most coming-out stories, Monette reveals as much about the times he grew up in as about himself.

***The Lost Language of Cranes*** by David Leavitt (319 pp.) This is a gay coming-of-age novel with a difference, for instead of focusing on the usual bar and bathhouse scene, Leavitt conjures up the mores of contemporary New York— the apartments and jobs, the schools and shops, the parties and chains of friendship. The odd twist here is that Philip, the hero, not only falls in love and gets his heart broken but also discovers that his father, too, is gay.

***Our Lady of the Flowers*** by Jean Genet (307 pp.) Written entirely in prison, this French classic is, according to Sartre (who adored it), a prolonged masturbatory fantasy. It's like a nightmare in which pimps, queens, sailors, and murderers swirl around the defeated and abandoned figure called Divine. Some find a violent poetry in Genet's surrealistic prose, others yearn for some grounding in plot and character. Either way, it's a provoking, utterly original book.

***Rubyfruit Jungle*** by Rita Mae Brown (217 pp.) This is a classic coming-of-age novel, narrated by a spunky tough-minded girl who comes of age lesbian in small-town Florida and later in New York City. What's remarkable about Molly is her utter lack of shame over her sexual identity—"sex with men is boring once you know what women are like" could be her motto. The many and varied sex scenes are funny, touching, and sure to incite discussion.

***The Object of My Affection*** by Stephen McCauley (316 pp.) McCauley's hero is a gay kindergarten teacher whose female roommate's pregnancy offers him a chance to have a family without sexual commitment. Some readers will no doubt find this book wishy-washy, while others will respect it as an honest appraisal of modern sexual confusion.

***Faggots*** by Larry Kramer (384 pp.) "There are 2,556,598 faggots in the New York City area," begins this funny, raunchy novel, and by the end you feel as if you've met about half of them. The hero Fred Lemish is about to turn forty and still looking for true love in Manhattan's bathhouses and on Fire Island. With its carefree, nonstop sex, this book now reads like a historical novel of the preAIDS era. You'll either love it or hate it.

***A Boy's Own Story*** by Edmund White (218 pp.) White's soft, mournful, elegiac style carries this volume of memoirs into a special category. Like *Becoming a Man,* this is a gay coming-of-age story, but less tortured. White's early, fumbling sexual encounters are sometimes funny, sometimes shocking, and always described with great tenderness and vividness. May provoke frank exchanges about sexual confusion and initiation.

***The Swimming-Pool Library*** by Alan Hollinghurst (336 pp.) Will, a recent Oxford graduate with a small independent income, sinks into a sybaritic London life of bars, clubs, sex cinemas, and public lavs, with lots of drink and quick one-offs. But torn between Arthur, the West Indian hiding from murder charges in his flat, and elderly Lord Nantwich, relic of an earlier generation, he must examine who he is and what he wants out of life. Erotic, intelligent, poignant, and unsparing.

# Aging

***Mrs. Stevens Hears the Mermaids Singing*** by May Sarton (220 pp.) A splendid choice for groups with older readers, this book centers on an interview with a female novelist, as she muses on her long life, her career, her various lovers (both male and female), and her garden. It doesn't attempt to sum up everything, but presents the mingled joys, regrets, and wisdom of a rich life.

***A Country Year: Living the Questions*** by Sue Hubbell (221 pp.) A commercial beekeeper in the Missouri Ozarks—fifty years old, divorced, her son grown and gone, just making ends meet—faces the second half of her life. Moving through the year, these lucid short essays explore work, day-to-day existence, the course of a woman's life, and nature (particularly bees) with self-reliance, wit, grace, and zest.

***The Book of Ebenezer Le Page*** by G. B. Edwards (394 pp.) A literary oddity, this is the author's only novel, begun when he was in his sixties and published after his death in 1976. Narrated by a crusty old Guernsey native (the glossary of Guernsey dialect is helpful), it's a protracted reminiscence of life in a Channel Island backwater, rife with local color and human detail. Funny, warm, endearing, and utterly original.

***To Dance with the White Dog*** by Terry Kay (178 pp.) Pecan farmer Sam Peek, after his beloved wife Cora dies, must learn to live on his own. His grown children swarm around, waiting to pick up the pieces of his life for him—until a mysterious white dog (that his kids can't see!) gives Sam new strength to live. Is the dog a stray, a hallucination, or his wife's ghost? This warm family comedy should appeal to readers of all ages.

# Nobelists

***Main Street*** by Sinclair Lewis (439 pp.) The United States' first Nobelist, Lewis was less a master of style and technique than a crusading social critic. Much of his social criticism is irrelevant today, but not this indictment of provincial narrow-mindedness, in which Carol Kennicott valiantly tries to bring culture to Gopher Prairie, Minnesota—and suffers for it.

***The Magic Mountain*** by Thomas Mann (716 pp.) A sanatorium for tuberculosis patients in Switzerland, on the brink of World War I, becomes the symbolic setting for the death of Europe. But this makes it sound terribly heavy, when in fact it's a rich world unto itself: sometimes funny, often tragic, always elegaic, with characters you'll care about as people, not just symbols. We felt like we'd been away for six months when we finished it.

***The Plague*** by Albert Camus (308 pp.) This 1947 parable of a city devastated by a mysterious plague strikes a chilling chord today, in a world shadowed by the AIDS epidemic. The writing, stripped of incidental detail, makes for grim but powerful reading. It may be too bleak for some groups' tastes, but those who are willing to be shaken up will certainly have something to talk about with this choice.

***The Solid Mandala*** by Patrick White (316 pp.) The duality of human nature is illustrated through the life story of twin brothers in Australia—small, clever, sarcastic Waldo, and large, dreamy, simpleminded Arthur. Their tale is told twice, once from each brother's wholly different perspective and in subtly different narrative voices. Sounds like a gimmick, but White really pulls it off.

***Molloy*** by Samuel Beckett (241 pp.) It's just what you'd expect from the author of *Waiting for Godot*—a desolate absurdist soliloquy with flashes of black humor. The physically immobile main character feels reality falling apart, and language becomes a mere buzzing in his head. Originally written in French (though Beckett was Irish, he settled in Paris), it requires attentive reading, but don't worry if it doesn't make perfect sense to you—it's not supposed to.

***Darkness Visible*** by William Golding (265 pp.) Even bleaker than *The Lord of the Flies,* this 1979 novel is less of a parable—it begins in the London blitz and ends with modern-day political terrorism. A small cast of disparate weirdos—a man deformed by bomb burns, a pederast schoolmaster, devious twin sisters, a bald old bookseller—eventually come together in a strange denouement. Some readers find it too depressing; others will enjoy wrestling with its dark truths about human nature.

***A Sport of Nature*** by Nadine Gordimer (354 pp.) Hillela, a white South African orphan cast out by her family, lives among political exiles, marries a black revolutionary, and rises to national prominence. Beautifully written but unflinching, it's an insightful study of a country where all lives are treacherously intermingled with politics.

## European Masters

***The Adventures of Don Quixote*** by Miguel de Cervantes Saavedra (various editions; Penguin edition 940 pp.) Cervantes's masterpiece is such a familiar cultural icon that you may be shocked at how very strange the original is: a masterful meld of humor and cruelty, high-flown rhetoric, and sheer narrative inventiveness. Compare this to the works of Shakespeare and Ben Jonson, who were Cervantes's contemporaries.

***Lost Illusions*** by Honore de Balzac (695 pp.) Balzac, like Dickens, packs all of society, from the haughtiest aristocrats to the lowest gutter rats, into his novels. This engrossing trilogy takes in the worlds of journalism, the stage, and the great noblewomen of Paris, with lots of complicated love affairs linking them all together. Start by analyzing the character of Balzac's hero Lucien Chardon.

***The Charterhouse of Parma*** by Stendhal (various editions; Penguin edition, 488 pp.) The petty complexities of Italian ducal politics, the impact of the Napoleonic Wars on European society, and the operatic loves of Stendhal's aristocratic hero Fabrizio combine to make this one of the great political novels of the nineteenth century. Is the *true* protagonist the unforgettable Duchessa Sanseverina?

***Crime and Punishment*** by Fyodor Dostoyevsky (various editions; Penguin edition, 559 pp.) Though this is a big book—try to allow two months' reading time—it's a taut, obsessive journey into the disordered mind and soul of a Russian intellectual who commits murder to prove a philosophical point. Or so he tells himself. Nightmarish, claustrophobic, totally engrossing, it's sure to provoke questions and emotions.

**Lady with Lapdog and Other Stories** by Anton Chekhov (281 pp.) What's astonishing about Chekhov is his range—from "Ward 6," about a doctor who ends up in the mental ward of his shabby hospital, to the title story about a casual adulterous affair that turns, unexpectedly, into a passionate obsession. The paradox of Chekhov is that he writes so richly and so subtly of utterly empty lives. The peerless artist of short fiction.

**Swann's Way** by Marcel Proust (325 pp.) The first volume of the monumental, seven-volume *Remembrance of Things Past* is the most accessible—there was even a recent film starring Jeremy Irons about the central episode, Swann's insane passion for Odette. But beware: Proust drives many readers to distraction with his endless sentences and infinite refinement. Defenders praise the detailed way he renders the play of human consciousness—but does one really want to dwell inside this particular mind?

**Buddenbrooks** by Thomas Mann (595 pp.) Mann published this family chronicle when he was only twenty-six, yet it is a fully realized work, tracing the decline of a rich burgher family in the north of Germany. Mann brings a modern ironic sensibility to the great themes of nineteenth-century literature—bad marriages, the getting and wasting of money, the oppressions of the past. It's hard to believe that this writer got even better later.

**The Complete Stories** by Franz Kafka (486 pp.) If you've only read *The Trial* and "The Metamorphosis," you're in for some wonderful surprises—the bizarre humor of "The Burrow," about a creature who seals himself in a kind of bunker and then listens for noises in the wall; "A Hunger Artist," in which fasting becomes a symbol for artistic performance; and the short fables—"A Fratricide," "The Problem of Our Laws," and "Poseidon," among the more notable. So what does "Kafkaesque" really mean?

**Auto-da-Fe** by Elias Canetti (464 pp.) Haunting and horrifying, this 1935 novel traces the descent into madness of a bibliophile who is swindled out of his precious library by his crafty housekeeper/wife. You can read this as a parable about the rise of totalitarianism, a savage commentary on the fate of European intellectuals, or even a portrait of a diseased marriage. Overwhelming and utterly original.

**History, A Novel** by Elsa Morante (555 pp.) Morante's "history" zeros in on one family—a mother, her children, her epileptic youngest child, a beloved dog—crushed by the horrors of World War II in Rome. The book is slow and weighted with particulars, but finally overwhelmingly tragic. Impossible to finish without crying. The topic of the Italians' ambivalent tolerance of Jews and ambivalent hatred of Nazis is worth pursuing.

**Invisible Cities** by Italo Calvino (165 pp.) Marco Polo sits in a garden with the aging emperor Kublai Khan and conjures up for his host images of fantastic, impossible cities—Diomira, with its sixty silver domes; Octavia, the spiderweb city; Moriana of the alabaster gates. Is this a plotless novel? A series of prose poems? A meditation on the soul of Venice? You will either be mesmerized by Calvino's imagination or you'll dismiss this as pretentious fluff.

**Confessions of Zeno** by Italo Svevo (398 pp.) This modernist masterpiece is narrated by a self-absorbed, unintentionally funny little man from Trieste. Zeno's "confessions" center on his lifelong search for health and happiness—in marriage, in love affairs, in business, by trying to quit smoking, through psychoanalysis. James Joyce, who knew Svevo in Trieste, was clearly influenced by his gift for capturing the ironies of everyday life.

## The Victorians

***Barchester Towers*** by Anthony Trollope (various editions; Penguin edition, 449 pp.) The second and best-known of Trollope's series of Barsetshire novels, this satire on Victorian church politics is brought to life by Trollope's skewering caricatures of English "types"—less broad than Dickens (you'll grin rather than laugh out loud), but nonetheless deliciously devastating.

***Middlemarch*** by George Eliot (various editions; Penguin edition, 838 pp.) A skillfully interwoven plot contrasts four provincial English young ladies and the marriages they make—for money, for status, for self-fulfillment, and only rarely for love. Eliot's a real grown-up's novelist, understanding all too well how lives go forever astray. A book that every woman should read—and reread every ten years or so.

***Wuthering Heights*** by Emily Brontë (various editions; Penguin edition, 367 pp.) This intensely focused novel set on the Yorkshire moors gave literature two of its all-time great lovers: Cathy and Heathcliff. Simplified in its movie versions, the plot is actually a complex puzzle of love played out in three generations; semimystical, wildly romantic, and psychologically acute, it opens up on endless levels, all of them fascinating.

***Our Mutual Friend*** by Charles Dickens (various editions; Penguin edition, 892 pp.) One of Dickens's later novels, it has wickedly penetrating comic caricatures, sympathetic protagonists, a delicate and melancholy love story, and a satiric theme that speaks to our age—it's all about money. Rather than reread one of the Dickens standards, why not try this neglected masterpiece?

***Vanity Fair*** by William Thackeray (various editions; Penguin edition, 797 pp.) A merciless satire—sometimes dated, sometimes wildly funny—this novel is a reading group favorite largely because of its heroine, Becky Sharp. Social climber, fortune hunter, and backstabber extraordinaire, she's one of English literature's most memorable characters. You could spend an entire evening arguing whether Thackeray despised her or really loved her in spite of himself.

***Jude the Obscure*** by Thomas Hardy (various editions; Penguin edition, 491 pp.) It's not *Lady Chatterley's Lover,* but you can still see why Hardy shocked the late Victorians with his frank discussion of human sexuality, as Jude's illicit passion for his cousin Sue threads together this darkly tragic tale. Some women's groups may prefer Hardy's brilliant *Tess of the D'Urbervilles,* but Jude and Sue—educated, "liberated" misfits in rural England—speak more to modern readers than Tess does.

***The Moonstone*** by Wilkie Collins (various editions; Penguin edition, 526 pp.) One of literature's first detective novels, this book zigzags throughout the ranks of society as it unravels the search for a missing diamond. It's relatively short by Victorian standards, and Collins—a close friend of Dickens—keeps suspense taut throughout, with a few sly flashes of humor.

***Dracula*** by Bram Stoker (various editions; Penguin edition, 486 pp.) Forget all the movie, TV, theater, and comic book versions you've seen—Stoker's 1897 original is a chilling Gothic masterpiece. Though it sometimes moves slowly, bear with it; old Fangs himself takes on a lot more depth. In your discussion, you can have a heyday with analyzing the Freudian subtext.

# There'll Always Be an England

***Precious Bane*** by Mary Webb (356 pp.) This 1926 minor English classic is set on an isolated farm in rural Shropshire, with a harelipped heroine—imagine Edith Wharton's *Ethan Frome* as written by Thomas Hardy and D. H. Lawrence, and you get the idea. Vivid characterizations and a wonderful eye for nature transform what would otherwise be a grimly moralistic tale. As a companion piece, try Stella Gibbons's sly parody *Cold Comfort Farm.*

***Howards End*** by E. M. Forster (288 pp.) Okay, so everyone has seen the film, one of the best (and most faithful) literary movies ever. It's still worth clearing your minds to read the original. Two families—the intellectual, freethinking Schlegels and the commercial, conservative Wilcoxes—are bound together by Mrs. Wilcox's bequest of her family home, Howards End, an embodiment of all that is English. Which force will win? This is a novel that stays with you for life.

***Living*** by Henry Green (175 pp.) Considered a master of prose style in England, Green was virtually out of print in the States until a recent revival. This 1929 novel about Birmingham factory workers has a very cinematic style—short takes, jump cuts, snatches of dialogue in thick Midlands dialect. Green, born an aristocrat, knew the milieu—he worked at his family's factory and boarded in a working-class home. Whether you discuss his politics or his artistic technique, you'll be engrossed.

***The Go-Between*** by L. P. Hartley (281 pp.) Edwardian England is elegiacally evoked as a man in his sixties recalls a childhood visit to a Norfolk country house. An undercurrent of sexual passion—the boy innocently carries messages for a young couple having an affair—gives the book a marvelous brooding atmosphere.

*A Fairly Honourable Defeat* by Iris Murdoch (447 pp.) A delightful, dialogue-crammed novel about a small set of Londoners bound by intricate webs of friendship and sexual attraction; happily married Rupert and Hilda and her sister Morgan are the central figures. Also a philosopher, Murdoch may be expounding theories about good and evil as the characters war for power over each other, but these never get in the way of an absorbing read.

*Waterland* by Graham Swift (358 pp.) Tom Crick—a middle-aged history teacher born of a family of storytellers—spins this engrossing tale of his youth in the East Anglia fens, with lots of fen-country history and ancestral anecdotes thrown in for good measure. Like the fens themselves, the book is dark rather than sunny; strands of violence and madness run throughout. Complex but entirely readable, it'll give you a lot to talk about.

*London Fields* by Martin Amis (470 pp.) This is the best book to date by Amis, possibly Britain's best contemporary writer. Peopled with louts, touts, and tarts, his London is a money-mad, loveless, violent place, and some readers may find this bleak murder novel hard to take. But his prose style is exquisite and his criticisms of Thatcherite England are pretty hard to ignore.

*The Child in Time* by Ian McEwan (263 pp.) A married couple's life unravels after their young daughter is stolen from them on the street. McEwan's understanding of emotional isolation and his willingness to face heartbreak dead-on make this an uncanny, powerful book. Yes, there's a happy ending, but maybe not what you'd expect—group members may disagree over whether it successfully resolves the book's conflicts.

# Through Irish Eyes

*A Portrait of the Artist as a Young Man* by James Joyce (253 pp.) Family, school, church, and Ireland all leave their marks on Stephen Dedalus as he grows from a toddler to a man. Joyce's dense, stream-of-consciousness writing traces Stephen's perceptions with almost cinematic clarity; others have copied this technique since, but none so well. It's a stunning achievement—and still an easier read than Joyce's masterpiece *Ulysses*. Good lead-off question: Who is "the artist" of the title?

*The Lonely Passion of Judith Hearne* by Brian Moore (223 pp.) A plain Irish spinster with lace-curtain pretensions and a wee drinking problem is the focus of this haunting novel. It's a brilliant study of loneliness and self-delusion, likely to trigger your group into sharing some soul-searching reflections.

*The Silence in the Garden* by William Trevor (204 pp.) Written by a master of the short story (he's published frequently in the *New Yorker*), this jewellike short novel depicts the last generation of a well-off Irish family, crumbling from years of hiding an awful guilty secret. Though the secret itself is anticlimactic, by the time it's revealed you've been won over by the melancholy atmosphere and sadly eccentric characters.

*The Snapper* by Roddy Doyle (216 pp.) Sharon Rabbitte, pregnant and unmarried, is the talk of her working-class Dublin neighborhood—Who's the dad?, everyone wonders. But Sharon's not talking, and her own dad surprises everyone by becoming her staunchest supporter. This novel is heavy on dialogue—in a thick Dublin accent, full of crass slang—but get past that and you've got a frank, funny, joyous family portrait.

***The All of It*** by Jeanette Haien (145 pp.) An elderly Irish priest hears a deathbed confession of a sin so egregious he cannot ignore it. Swift, gripping, tightly focused, it's a story you might read in one sitting, but the moral issues it raises will definitely provide grist for group discussion. And it's a first novel, written by a concert pianist who only summers in Ireland—it shouldn't be this good, but it is.

***The Copper Beech*** by Maeve Binchy (407 pp.) Each chapter follows the life of a different resident of the village of Shancarrig; the pieces fall together like a puzzle, each person connected to the others in a vital chain of pivotal incidents. The range of types resembles any small town, though issues of religion and class have a particularly Irish ring to them. It's an easy read, a life-affirming book with characters you'll care about.

## The New Englanders

***The House of the Seven Gables*** by Nathaniel Hawthorne (various editions; Penguin edition, 319 pp.) In an old wooden house in Salem, Massachusetts, the last members of the Pyncheon family live under the family curse, brought on by a Puritan ancestor who had his neighbor hung for witchcraft. Can sweet young cousin Phoebe cancel the family doom? Pitiful, poignant, darkly romantic, this book is even more intriguing if you can spot the parallels to Hawthorne's own life.

***Moby-Dick*** by Herman Melville (various editions; Penguin edition, 625 pp.) Allow two months for this monster. The self-effacing narrator ("Call me Ishmael") signs on with mysterious Captain Ahab for a whaling voyage like no other. The great white whale they're chasing is obviously a symbol, but the big question is: A symbol for what? No two critics agree, so have fun hashing it out. *Note:* You could skip the various chapters on whaling technique, but some readers think they're the best part.

**Walden** by Henry Thoreau (various editions; Penguin edition, 382 pp.) Philosopher, rebel, and a bit of a crank, Henry Thoreau ditched society for two years to live in a cabin by a pond in the woods. Vigorous, deft writing and keen observations of nature make this wandering essay a delight, but Thoreau's personality so permeates the book that discussion will inevitably focus on the man himself. It's easy to see why it was passionately read in the 1960s; does it still hold meaning for our end of the century?

**Country of the Pointed Firs** by Sarah Orne Jewett (133 pp.) This loosely connected series of sketches set in a coastal Maine town in the late nineteenth century celebrates the women who carry on while their menfolk go off to sea. Jewett's constant use of dialect—a staple in the "local color" school of which she was queen—annoys some readers; others get involved with the characters so quickly they stop noticing. Willa Cather was deeply influenced by Jewett; compare their work.

**The Bostonians** by Henry James (various editions; Penguin edition, 390 pp.) A look at the nineteenth-century women's movement, set amidst the earnest, genteel reformers of polite Boston society. James serves up his customary subtle perceptions and delicate irony, but (blessedly) this is in his earlier, clearer prose style. James wrote this ten years after leaving Boston to live in Europe—reading it, can you understand why he went?

**The Outermost House** by Henry Beston (222 pp.) Like Thoreau, Henry Beston wrote about a year lived alone in a cabin, this one being on a Cape Cod beach. The difference between this and *Walden* lies in Beston's spirit—reverent, gently precise, humbled by nature. A lyrical masterpiece of nature description, this book will tempt you to read aloud (and maybe inspire you to spend next summer on the Cape!).

*A Prayer for Owen Meany* by John Irving (617 pp.) A Vietnam draft evader/long resident in Canada looks back on his New Hampshire boyhood and his best friend: tiny, precocious Owen Meany, an unlikely and thoroughly endearing hero. Like other Irving novels, it's full of eccentric characters, orphans of various kinds, and sudden tragedies. On another level, it may also be a political history and a spiritual journey—depending on whether or not you think Irving shares his narrator's opinions.

*The Beans of Egypt, Maine* by Carolyn Chute (238 pp.) The Bean family is a sloppy white-trash clan living in a mobile home next door to Earlene Pomerleau; it takes a while to get all the Beans straight, but as they become individuals, we start to care about their feuds, tics, and inarticulate loves. Portraits this authentic-feeling *have* to be drawn from life—though her humor's never corrosive or mean, we wonder how Chute's neighbors feel when she writes about them.

*Postcards* by E. Annie Proulx (308 pp.) Several scrawled postcards to various members of the Blood family each set off a chapter in this saga of a farming family come to the end of the road. Proulx's rich, intricate narrative prose stands in refreshing counterpoint to the New Englanders' laconic dialogue.

*Vanished* by Mary McGarry Morris (246 pp.) In a small Vermont town, shy, married, middle-aged Aubrey Wallace suddenly runs off with a sexy teenager named Dotty; they pick up a stranger's child, whom they treat as their own, and embark on a startling road trip. Morris really goes for extremes of personality; her characters may make some people in your group uneasy, but others will be fascinated by their reckless abandon.

## Songs of the South

*Light in August* by William Faulkner (480 pp.) Challenging and multifaceted, this novel revolves around the figure of Joe Christmas—orphan, outcast, and killer—who assumes he is "a Negro," though he "passes" for white and has no idea who his parents are. Other mysteries abound, not the least of them why Faulkner chose this particular title. This is one book for which you may want to read some literary criticism.

*A Summons to Memphis* by Peter Taylor (209 pp.) Nobody else captures the nuances of the upper-middle-class South so well as Peter Taylor. The narrator of this novel returns to Memphis, Tennessee, to mediate a dispute between his sisters and their widowed father, who's planning to remarry. On this fragile base, Taylor builds a wise story of generational conflict, social rivalries, and the power of memory.

*The Optimist's Daughter* by Eudora Welty (208 pp.) Welty wrote this in a rush of inspiration after her mother died, and this, her most autobiographical work, reads like a tirade and a passionate summing-up. Laurel McKelva, the protagonist, sees her father die through the brutal carelessness of his flaky young second wife, and in her grief Laurel muses deeply on her troubled past. Compare to Peter Taylor.

*The Surface of Earth* by Reynolds Price (491 pp.) This is a big, sprawling family saga, spanning four decades in the history of two North Carolina families. Price packs the narrative with major themes—a brief unhappy marriage that produces

Rob Mayfield, the bitter relationship between Rob and his mother, the death of Rob's wife, Rob's strained love for his son, and his dependence on the affection and trust of black people. Some readers find it cloying; others declare this a masterpiece.

***Bastard Out of Carolina*** by Dorothy Allison (309 pp.) Bone, the (female) bastard of the title, narrates her harrowing life story up to the age of thirteen—a story of sexual abuse, drunken uncles, hard women, and dead-end lives in Greenville, South Carolina, in the 1950s. It sounds like just another Southern Gothic but Allison doesn't hit a single false note.

***Three by Flannery O'Connor*** by Flannery O'Connor (447 pp.) A collection of her finest work—the short novels "Wise Blood" and "The Violent Bear It Away" and the story series *A Good Man Is Hard to Find*. O'Connor's blistering mix of black humor, Catholicism, and Southern grotesquerie is not for everyone. But even if you're put off by her maimed evangelists, predatory mothers, and wooden-legged daughters, you've got to admit she's a true original.

***Reflections in a Golden Eye*** by Carson McCullers (140 pp.) Why did the Gothic style flower so luxuriantly in the South? However you answer this question, use this novel as one of your prime illustrations. It is the story of a perverse love triangle between the fussy Captain Penderton, his luscious feeble-minded wife Leonora, and a slim young soldier who loves to ride horses naked in the sun. A brilliant study of bizarre obsession.

***Cold Sassy Tree*** by Olive Ann Burns (391 pp.) Spunky young Will Tweedy narrates this story of his recently widowed grandfather, whose second marriage to a bold young woman with a secret past scandalizes the whole family—and the whole town. This portrait of small-town Georgia at the turn of the century is a whopping good read, with a lively, funny, and utterly believable narrative voice.

***Paris Trout*** by Pete Dexter (306 pp.) Cotton Point, Georgia, is stunned by the cruel murder of a black child by miserly Paris Trout; lawyer Harry Seagraves, hired to defend Trout, finds his own life turned upside down in the process. A book about race, class, small towns, and thwarted passion, it's tense, atmospheric, and absorbing.

## Writers from the Heartland

***Indian Summer*** by William Dean Howells (267 pp.) Ohio native Howells is better known for his masterpiece of social realism *The Rise of Silas Lapham,* but this finely ironic comedy in the Henry James vein speaks more to us today. Set in Italy, it's about a "middle-aged" (actually, in his late thirties!) newspaper editor from small-town Indiana, revisiting the scene of his youthful Grand Tour and getting caught in a delicate love triangle.

***The Magnificent Ambersons*** by Booth Tarkington (324 pp.) Though very much a period piece, Tarkington's dissection of the upper social strata in a midwest city—Indianapolis in the teens and twenties—still works as nostalgic comedy. His best characters are the young adults, courting and choosing careers, oblivious to the disappointments of their elders. Convince group members not to see the masterful Orson Welles film version until *after* they've read the book.

***An American Romance*** by John Casey (321 pp.) The complicated, on-again-off-again love affair of Mac and Anya sprawls sexily through Casey's first novel, supplying the book's power and suspense. These are real, fully rounded, flawed characters, mired in the particulars of Iowa in the days when young artistic people still lived in communes. Casey is especially good on the tension between midwest roots and the lure of New York.

***Great Plains*** by Ian Frazier (290 pp.) "A person can be amazingly happy on the Great Plains," writes Frazier in this information-packed joy ride through the short-grass big sky country of the Dakotas and Montana all the way down to Texas. Frazier is the ideal traveling companion—chatty, skeptical, funny, and tireless in his pursuit of oddball places like the site of Sitting Bull's camp or Lawrence Welk's North Dakota hometown.

***Giants in the Earth*** by O. E. Rolvaag (453 pp.) Heartbreaking and stark, this is truly an epic, about a family from Norway braving the hardships of pioneer life in the 1870s. Rolvaag makes his hero and heroine equally vivid—Per Hansa, the father, bursts with enthusiasm, energy, and boundless hope for the future, while his wife Beret goes slowly mad amid the endless empty expanses. The blizzards and grasshopper plagues are unforgettable.

***My Ántonia*** by Willa Cather (238 pp.) We watch the lovely, full-blooded Ántonia Shimerda, daughter of immigrants from Bohemia, grow up through the eyes of her young neighbor Jim Burden. Part coming-of-age novel, part paean to the Nebraska prairies, it's full of lyrical nature description and fine-tuned characterization. Read it less for plot than for atmosphere and evocation of an era forever past.

***Time Will Darken It*** by William Maxwell (375 pp.) A neglected masterpiece, this is a haunting novel of a marriage unraveling under the weight of passion, one hot summer in a small midwestern town. It's best read in long stretches, so you

can fall under its nostalgic spell. Lyrically written and merci-
lessly true, it invites discussion on many levels.

***Lake Wobegon Days*** by Garrison Keillor (337 pp.) Small-
town America is celebrated in this "history" of a mythical
Minnesota town. You may think you've heard it all in Keillor's
"A Prairie Home Companion" radio monologues, but give this
a serious read: it says a lot about what Middle Americans hold
sacred, and why. And the writing's an unexpected joy—funny,
warmhearted, beautifully modulated, nostalgic—you may find
yourselves laughing out loud.

***Aquamarine*** by Carol Anshaw (197 pp.) A former Olympic
swimming medalist from Missouri faces her dwindled life
twenty-two years later— or rather, three possible parallel lives
(the old "two roads diverged in a yellow wood" idea). The
amazing thing is how much the central character stays the
same in these utterly different and totally believable scenarios.
Very much a woman's book, though neither sentimental nor
stridently feminist.

## Western Voices

***All the Pretty Horses*** by Cormac McCarthy (302 pp.)
McCarthy takes up all the conventions of the western—the
lonesome cowboy, the ravishing Mexican beauty, the worship
of horses, the endless rides through parched terrain—and si-
multaneously explodes and enshrines them. It's quite a feat. It
is also, like all of McCarthy's books, soaked in blood—which
raises the question of the esthetic impact of violence.

***A River Runs Through It*** by Norman Maclean (217 pp.) All
you ever wanted to know about fly fishing. In passing, however, the narrator tells us so much about his father, his brother,

and himself (as well as their relationships to various women) that the sport becomes a metaphor for life as a man. Why is the faithful, reverent film version directed by Robert Redford so wooden while the book is so deeply engrossing?

***A Lady's Life in the Rocky Mountains*** by Isabella L. Bird (256 pp.) A middle-aged English gentlewoman, finding herself in the Colorado Rockies in the autumn and early winter of 1873, wrote this vivid, arresting series of letters about her adventures. Traveling alone on horseback, Isabella Bird must have struck the mountain men and miners as a creature from another planet. But what's really fascinating here is how *they* struck *her*.

***Death Comes for the Archbishop*** by Willa Cather (343 pp.) Cather beautifully evokes the land and the native peoples of the Southwest in this novel based on the actual career of Archbishop Remy, who came to Santa Fe as a young priest and died many years later a powerful archbishop. Beneath the serene surface lie thorny moral questions about the nature of friendship, the sacrifices faith exacts, and relations between the Spanish, Native Americans, and Anglos.

***This House of Sky*** by Ivan Doig (314 pp.) Doig opens his beautiful memoir of growing up in the back country of Montana with his earliest memory: the death of his mother when he was six. A lonely childhood in the care of his father, a former ranchhand, gives Doig an extraordinary sensitivity to the Montana landscape and the people who live amid its stern distances. Interesting to compare this with Maclean's *A River Runs Through It*.

***Bless Me, Ultima*** by Rudolfo A. Anaya (248 pp.) Written by a Chicano who grew up in Santa Rosa, New Mexico, this novel vividly conveys the texture of life as it has been lived for generations in the American Southwest—the blending of

Catholicism and folk superstition, the sway of the sun over the landscape, the power of family. At the center of the story is the enigmatic figure of Ultima, a kind of benign witch, who initiates the young narrator into life's beauty and mystery.

**The Good Rain** by Timothy Egan (254 pp.) Egan, the Pacific Northwest correspondent for *The New York Times,* roams his beat for intriguing subjects—the sorry state of the Puyallup Indian tribe; a hike up Mount Rainier to scatter his grandfather's ashes; the elusive Fred Beckey, mountain goat of the North Cascades. Along the way he throws in helpings of history, local color, and reflections on the pressures bearing down on this lush corner of the country.

**Housekeeping** by Marilynne Robinson (219 pp.) Set in a damp, mountainous corner of the northwest, this haunting first novel is about two sisters: Ruth, the narrator, who's cut from the same cloth as her mother (a suicide) and her hobo aunt Sylvie; and Lucille, who battles the family eccentricity by opting for the "normal" life of an American teenager. What matters in this book is not its plot but its dreamlike mood.

**Play It As It Lays** by Joan Didion (213 pp.) Didion uses the scalpel of her pared-down prose to open up the mind of Maria Wyeth, an actress-model-whatever on her way down in the jittery Hollywood of the 1960s. The anomie feels somewhat dated now—the aimless freeway cruising, the drugs, the jaunts to Vegas—but the book still casts a spell. Some will find this as irresistible as gossip, others may feel it's just as empty. A quick read.

## Latin American Masters

***Kiss of the Spider Woman*** by Manuel Puig (281 pp.) Puig's highly charged Argentine novel about the prison relationship of a gay window dresser and a dedicated revolutionary has inspired a movie and a musical, but the book is both more powerful and more complex than the spin-offs. Writing entirely in dialogue (along with erudite footnotes), Puig weaves in issues of morality, politics, fantasy, gender and sexual orientation, and cinematic iconography.

***Labyrinths*** by Jorge Luis Borges (287 pp.) You could devote most of your evening to trading favorite bits of these short prose pieces—Tlon, the imaginary "third world" in which time and space are negated; the story of a man obsessed with rewriting *Don Quixote*; the notes for a story about the enigmatic murder of Kilpatrick, "secret and glorious captain of conspirators." Borges's tone is strangely reminiscent of Poe, but a Poe wittily obsessed with obscure books.

***The Time of the Hero*** by Mario Vargas Llosa (409 pp.) Peruvian master Vargas Llosa set his first novel in the tense, claustrophobic world of a military academy in Lima. A group of boys forms an inner circle, complete with sadistic initiation rites; a petty theft they casually commit leads to murder and suicide. You can approach this as a commentary on the violence of adolescence, or place it in the context of other Latin American fictions.

***The Lost Steps*** by Alejo Carpentier (278 pp.) In this haunting novel by a gifted Cuban stylist, a composer weary of civilization flees New York and plunges into the timeless wilderness along a South American river. Carpentier interweaves musings on history, time, and anthropology, allusions to *The Odyssey*, and musical metaphors to create a vibrant narrative. Intellectually provocative, but written in clear, accessible prose.

***Leopoldina's Dream*** by Silvina Ocampo (204 pp.) The title story in this collection is about an old woman who has the power to dream objects into existence—and it's narrated by her lapdog. This gives you some idea of the surreal, deceptively simple conceits this Argentine writer plays with. Comparisons with Borges and García Marquez spring to mind, but Ocampo is more of a moralist, scrutinizing the interrelations between heaven and hell. It's noteworthy that she studied to be a painter.

***The Old Gringo*** by Carlos Fuentes (199 pp.) Mexican writer Fuentes spent years pondering the mysterious disappearance of American satirist Ambrose Bierce in Mexico, eventually writing this novel in which he imagines how the "old gringo" died. Interwoven with a meditation on Bierce's career is the story of a love affair between a proud American woman and a doomed Mexican general—a symbol, perhaps, for the passionate love/hate relationship between Mexico and the United States.

***House of the Spirits*** by Isabel Allende (448 pp.) Chronicling the generations of an aristocratic Chilean family, this dreamlike novel somehow becomes more real than your own life while you're reading it. After the group is done exchanging favorite scenes and characters, settle down to comparing this to the works of other "magical realists" like Gabriel García Marquez and Mario Vargas Llosa. Why did this literary technique flower in South America and not North?

## Writers of Color

***Brothers and Keepers*** by John Edgar Wideman (243 pp.) A harrowing and true tale of two contemporary African-American brothers—the author, who "made good" as a writer and college teacher, and his youngest brother, Robby, imprisoned for life for armed robbery and murder. Wideman alternates his own thoughtful narration with tense, angry letters from his brother in jail. This stunning, heartbreaking book raises difficult issues about race, family relations, and America's justice system.

*I Know Why the Caged Bird Sings* by Maya Angelou (281 pp.) In lyrical, subtle prose, poet Angelou tells of her harsh, magical, painfully brief childhood. Whether she's writing about the "African-bush secretiveness" of her strong grandmother, about being raped at age eight, or about becoming an unwed mother at sixteen, her marvelous restrained strength shines through. By the book's end, you feel as if you've made a wonderful new friend.

*The Color Purple* by Alice Walker (251 pp.) Though this book is told in two voices, it is Celie—a slow, homely, ignorant sharecropper's daughter—whose tale will captivate you, overshadowing the pallid counterpoint of her missionary sister Nettie's account of Africa. This book is less about race relations than about relations between the sexes—men will have to defend themselves against Walker's scathing depictions.

*Waiting to Exhale* by Terry McMillan (400 pp.) The lives and loves of the black middle class, engagingly told by a sassy quartet of women friends. Bound together by their mutual search for a good man, these women hold strong to their families, their careers, and their sisterhood. Less "literary" than Toni Morrison or Alice Walker, McMillan is also more accessible for whites. Is that this book's strength or its weakness?

*Their Eyes Were Watching God* by Zora Neale Hurston (184 pp.) Hurston's vivid depiction of African-American rural life in Florida threw black literary stereotypes out the window when it was published in 1937. Though the dialect seems dated, the cast of strong, complex women and men makes the book unforgettable. Comparisons with Alice Walker, who rediscovered Hurston, will get discussion moving; then consider whether Hurston was a feminist.

**The Middle Passage** by Charles Johnson (209 pp.) Johnson's award-winning novel about the slave trade is so powerfully imagined that one can't help wishing it were better. Rutherford Calhoun, a freed slave and a scoundrel, narrates a vivid tale of life aboard a slaving ship, but then a clumsy, redemption-through-love story gets in the way. Still, lots of moral issues to discuss. Question: How credible is Calhoun's narrative voice?

**Daughters** by Paule Marshall (408 pp.) This is one of those novels you just want to curl up with—a long, leisurely, minutely observed story about the crises and joys of Ursa MacKenzie, a highly educated, deeply caring black woman struggling to make a good life for herself in today's New York. Episodes set on the imaginary Caribbean island of Triunion, where Ursa was born, add depth and contrast. Would one read the book in the same way if the characters were white?

**Having Our Say** by the Delany Sisters (210 pp.) Two sisters—101-year-old Bessie, a dentist, and 103-year-old Sadie, a high school teacher—look back over their astonishing lives, from their childhood in Raleigh's most prominent black family to front-row seats on the Harlem Renaissance. Candor, spunk, and down-to-earth humor make them endearing companions for a ride through the twentieth century.

## Poetry Picks

***Leaves of Grass*** by Walt Whitman (Rinehart edition, 472 pp.) If you suffered through Whitman in college, you might be surprised at how deeply you'll admire him now (then again, you might not). "Song of Myself" remains utterly fresh—and strange—and one can only wonder what they made of it in 1855. Focus on the great ones—"I Sing the Body Electric," "Song of the Open Road," "Crossing Brooklyn Ferry."

***The Complete Poems 1927–1979*** by Elizabeth Bishop (287 pp.) For years critics slotted Bishop as a miniaturist with a knack for precise description. But her stock has soared since then, and she's now recognized as a poet of quiet power and fierce restraint. Recent revelations about her alcoholism and lesbianism have changed the way we read such masterpieces as "The Man-Moth" and "Crusoe in England." The Brazil poems are all superb.

***Diving Into the Wreck*** by Adrienne Rich (62 pp.) Rich began her career writing in the great male lyric tradition, but she tore herself free from everything male and traditional in this break-through volume. "The freedom of the wholly mad/to smear & play with her madness," one furious poem opens. Rich, a wife and mother, became a symbol for radical feminism in the 1970s when she declared herself a lesbian, but these are not the poems of a "spokesperson"—only of a brilliant poet in agony.

***Lunch Poems*** by Frank O'Hara (74 pp.) Our chattiest, most likable poet. Reading these poems is like eavesdropping on the life of gay Greenwich Village in the 1950s—but anyone who has tried to adopt this intimate, immediate, conversational style knows how hard it is not to sound cute (even O'Hara had trouble keeping it up for long). Comparisons with

Whitman, William Carlos Williams, and even Allen Ginsberg are in order.

**High Windows** by Philip Larkin (42 pp.) Larkin was the curmudgeon of contemporary English lyric poets—"one of those old-type *natural* fouled-up guys," as he imagines his future biographer calling him. He rails against the litter of England in decline, but his rare moments of tenderness (expressed through gritted teeth) are all the more touching.

**Life Studies** by Robert Lowell (90 pp.) In this fierce volume of poems and a long autobiographical essay, Lowell threw off his knotty, tortured early style and made confessional poetry a household term. Would we care as much about Lowell's madness and horrible parents if he had not been one of *the* Lowells? Is confessional verse just a fancy term for self-indulgence?

**Poems 1965–1975** by Seamus Heaney (228 pp.) The wet earth smell of his native Ireland pervades Heaney's verse, and the tragedy of Irish politics weighs heavily, especially in the later poems. But for all the raw violence of his imagery, Heaney is ultimately a gentle, forgiving poet who wears the dark mantle of his time reluctantly. Read him aloud (preferably with a brogue) to appreciate his perfect pitch.

**Love Poems** by Anne Sexton (68 pp.) Searing, frank, desperate, naked, these poems crave and celebrate female sexual fulfillment. They set the poetry world on its ear when they were published in 1969. "The Ballad of the Lonely Masturbator," "In Celebration of My Uterus," "For My Lover, Returning to His Wife"—the titles alone will fire your discussion. Read the Diane Middlebrook biography and ponder Sexton's suicide.

## Nonfiction Picks

*In Cold Blood* by Truman Capote (343 pp.) A Kansas family is brutally murdered in their home by a pair of warped drifters. True crime has never been rendered in more precise, lyrical, evocative prose, but Capote's real achievement is how completely he enters into the minds of the convicted killers. In his obsessively thorough research, did he lose perspective on the horror of the crime? A disturbing and fascinating book.

*From Beirut to Jerusalem* by Thomas Friedman (526 pp.) A Pulitzer Prize-winning reporter for *The New York Times* elucidates the whole Middle East mess for the ordinary reader. On-the-spot anecdotes of life in a danger zone (Friedman was the *Times'* bureau chief in both cities of the title) lead into background discussion about the region's culture and tangled political history. Friedman is a scholar, a storyteller, *and* a clear thinker—what a rare combination!

*There Are No Children Here* by Alex Kotlowitz (305 pp.) This *Wall Street Journal* reporter spent two years getting inside the lives of Lafeyette and Pharoah, a pair of brothers growing up in a less-than-model Chicago housing project. This understated, quietly harrowing book makes issues such as urban decay, violence, and the failed welfare system suddenly very personal—and impossible to sweep under the carpet. Now it's up to us to discuss solutions.

*Backlash* by Susan Faludi (552 pp.) The media went wild for this surprise best-seller about the "backlash" that derailed the women's movement in the 1980s. If you believe what you read, this book—along with the Clarence Thomas hearings—set off a "genderquake" that galvanized female consciousness and activism once again. Do you believe this book had such an effect? Do you believe this book, period? Come prepared for a brawl.

*A Natural History of the Senses* by Diane Ackerman (309 pp.) Ackerman, a poet and a nature writer, pulls off quite a feat—in five long chapters, one on each of the senses, she explores various sensory experiences and our historical and cultural associations with them. No plot, no characters, but lots of fascinating facts and observations, woven together with some beautiful passages of pure description. Some members may ask "What's the point?", others will defend it to the death.

*The Hero Within* by Carol Pearson (196 pp.) Why is this personal growth self-help book a worthy reading group selection? Perhaps because Pearson drew from Joseph Campbell's masterful book on mythology, *The Hero with a Thousand Faces,* in delineating the six archetypes she believes we base our self-images upon—and in describing these archetypes, she often refers to models from literature. Women's groups in particular seem to respond to Pearson's thoughtful, intelligent system for self-analysis.

*Refuge: An Unnatural History of Family and Place* by Terry Tempest Williams (290 pp.) As the Great Salt Lake threatens Utah ecology by rising higher and higher, Williams—a naturalist—also watches her mother slowly succumb to cancer, a result of 1950s atomic bomb testing to which she too was exposed. The writing is spare, quiet, heartfelt, the evocation of Colorado Basin landscapes finely observed. It's a poignant meditation on nature, on grief, and on mortality.

*The Great War and Modern Memory* by Paul Fussell (363 pp.) World War I could be called "the most literary of wars," since so many gifted poets fought (and died) in it. Fussell, a literary critic, examines this war and its literature, then goes on to discourse on the ways in which "real life" and literary tradition transect. For added poignancy, read *Men Who March Away,* a collection of poetry by World War I soldiers such as Wilfred Owen, Rupert Brooke, Robert Graves, and Siegfried Sassoon.

***The Fatal Shore: The Epic of Australia's Founding*** by Robert Hughes (628 pp.) This really is an epic, at least in length, with hundreds of pages crammed with facts about the British system of transporting convicts overseas that led to the colonization of Australia. The weight of detail may crush some readers, but the portraits of the convicts are harrowing.

***Solitude*** by Anthony Storr (216 pp.) It may strike some as strange to talk about solitude in so unsolitary a setting as a book group, but Storr's book about the creative uses of solitude is packed with fascinating ideas, as well as telling character sketches of lonely geniuses like Henry James, Wittgenstein, and Beatrix Potter. When you tire of analysis, swap stories about your own favorite solitary moments.

## Nature and the Environment

***My First Summer in the Sierra*** by John Muir (272 pp.) Originally published in 1916, this rhapsodic account of a summer spent in the Yosemite region is still as fresh as paint today. Muir's work as a sheepherder left him free to botanize, observe land formations, and soak in the wonders of "these vast, calm, measureless mountain days." It is impossible to read this book without feeling a desperate desire to follow in Muir's footsteps.

***A Sand County Almanac*** by Aldo Leopold (228 pp.) One of the classics of twentieth-century nature writing, this beautiful and vigorous book influenced Edward Abbey, Annie Dillard, and a host of others. Leopold writes of the changing seasons at his "Sand farm" in Wisconsin and of his impressions of natural places far afield. He adds forceful essays about conservation and the American attitudes toward wildlife, essays that will give you plenty to talk about.

**Desert Solitaire** by Edward Abbey (303 pp.) Abbey's account of his three seasons as park ranger in Arches National Monument in Utah is shot through with beauty, terror, crackpot theories, reflections on cowboys and Indians, keen-eyed observation, and a dreamlike voyage through the doomed Glen Canyon. Abbey doesn't gush: he is tough and crusty, balancing his love of the Southwest with his contempt for those who can't appreciate it.

**Coming Into the Country** by John McPhee (417 pp.) McPhee, an artist of nonfiction prose, fashions this narrative of contemporary Alaska by braiding together history, natural history, politics, acute observation of landscape and weather, and journals about his adventurous treks into the back country. Discussion might focus on McPhee's deceptively simple style, his choice of detail, or on the issues of wilderness, development, and human character that the book so eloquently raises.

**Beyond the Hundredth Meridian** by Wallace Stegner (438 pp.) John Wesley Powell is the central figure in this Stegner classic, yet the book is less biography than a study of a visionary explorer-scientist and his engagement with the arid lands west of the hundredth meridian (from the western Dakotas and Kansas all the way to the West Coast). Powell's recommendations for land use in the West were way ahead of his time—and ours too; the West is still paying the price of ignoring him.

**The Meadow** by James Galvin (230 pp.) Reverence for the remote high country of the Colorado Rockies pervades this serene book, which melds together fiction, natural history, and meditation into a seamless whole. Galvin, a poet, traces the struggles of the families who tried to live on one mountain meadow for a century, eloquently conveying the passage of time and season at 8,500 feet. This is a prose poem without any of the brooding pretension that so often weighs down that form.

**Arctic Dreams** by Barry Lopez (464 pp.) Lopez has the true nature writer's gift of combining mysticism with fact, curiosity with reverence. *Arctic Dreams* is both an education—about the habits of musk oxen and polar bears, about aurora borealis and solar rings, about voyages of discovery and the desires of the voyagers—and the drama of a very fine mind in the act of discovery. Discussions may veer off on tangents like ecology, anthropology, or adventure travel.

**Beautiful Swimmers** by William W. Warner (304 pp.) You'll never again eat a crab without recalling this superb account of how these elusive critters are caught in Chesapeake Bay. It's hard to know whom Warner stands more in awe of—the Atlantic blue crabs or the watermen who have pursued them ingeniously for generations. This beautifully written book conveys the fragility of both marine and human communities, without imposing a political agenda.

## Travelers

**Black Lamb and Grey Falcon** by Rebecca West (1,150 pp.) We cannot lie to you; this is one long book. But West's wry, swift, surefooted prose keeps it moving, and anyone who wants to know about that patched-together nation once called Yugoslavia has to read this account of her 1937 journey there, laced with histories of each of its constituent countries. She meant to help her own generation understand why World War

I started there; she helps us understand what's happening there today.

***The Great Railway Bazaar*** by Paul Theroux (342 pp.) A glorious ode to train travel speeds from London across Europe to Istanbul, then crosses Asia on several exotic train lines. Along the way, Theroux introduces us to a number of intriguing fellow-travelers—it's not the trains so much as the passengers that fascinate him in the end. Written with all his novelist's command of characterization, it's a wonderful armchair journey.

***On Persephone's Island*** by Mary Taylor Simeti (330 pp.) Simeti, an American expatriate and a wise and perceptive writer, first visited Sicily in 1962 and returned twenty years later to marry and settle there. This lovely book deftly interweaves history, mythology, family matters, bits of lore, observations of the seasons, literary allusions, and descriptions of wonderful foods. Revelations abound for those who think of Sicily solely as the home of the Mafia.

***The Stones of Florence*** by Mary McCarthy (230 pp.) Even if you've never been to Florence and never intend to go, this is a gem worth reading. Opinionated as always, McCarthy never wrote better than this; she combines history, art and architecture appreciation, tourist guidance, and sheer cussedness until it reads like a novel. The companion volume, *Venice Observed,* is not quite as good—but they're both short and could be read together for an evening of Italian delights.

***Old Glory*** by Jonathan Raban (408 pp.) Growing up in England, Raban fell in love with the Mississippi River from afar; now he takes us with him on a boat trip down the great river today, from Minneapolis to New Orleans. It's a highly entertaining look at America's heartland as seen by an enthusiastic outsider; Raban now lives in America, and you can guess why.

***In Patagonia*** by Bruce Chatwin (204 pp.) Traveling to the southern tip of South America, Chatwin interweaves snatches of history with modern-day description and anecdotes, as he hunts down the traces of his grandmother's sea-captain cousin who shipwrecked in the Straits of Magellan. Reveling in bleak landscapes and incongruous personalities, Chatwin draws us along with crisp, lucid, vividly visualized prose.

***Holidays in Hell*** by P. J. O'Rourke (257 pp.) Traveling to third-world hot spots and "darkest America" (i.e., Epcot Center and Heritage USA), humorist O'Rourke casts a jaundiced eye on everything. He's hardly an objective observer, since he's constantly diverted by his conservative politics, a self-dramatizing gonzo style, and compulsive joking. But funny he is, and there just might be some truth to what he sees.

***Video Night in Katmandu*** by Pico Iyer (374 pp.) An incredibly observant fly on the wall, Iyer travels throughout Asia recording the insidious infiltration of Western culture. Born in England, educated at Eton, Oxford, and Harvard, Iyer has just the right dry wit to let us see the absurdity for ourselves. But what are the political or historical ramifications of all this? Iyer prefers to let his readers argue that out themselves.

***Destinations*** by Jan Morris (242 pp.) Jan Morris describes herself, modestly, as a "middle-aged Anglo-Welsh writer of romantic instinct"—yet these essays reveal her as wonderfully quirky and funny as well, if sometimes a touch glib. Her focus here is on cities, from the "fearful beauty" of Manhattan to the explosive exhaustion of Cairo to childish macho symbols in Panama. The fact that she had a sex change has no bearing on her writing, but it's too fascinating to ignore.

# Biography

***The Life of Charlotte Brontë*** by Elizabeth Gaskell (623 pp.) Though long and slow to get started, this biography is definitely worth the effort. Brontë's tragic, repressed life still amazes us, a century and a half later, and Gaskell—herself a successful Victorian novelist—never softens or disguises the truth. Her portrayal of Brontë as a brave woman fighting for self-expression made this an early feminist classic.

***Eminent Victorians*** by Lytton Strachey (267 pp.) Bloomsburyite Strachey won his fame with these four biographical essays on major Victorian figures: Cardinal Manning, Florence Nightingale, educator Thomas Arnold, and General Gordon. His portraits are controversially unreliable, both as biography and as a commentary on Victorian society, but they sure do make lively reading. Which is more important: truth, or entertaining distortions? Get ready to argue.

***Henry James*** by Leon Edel (740 pp.) James fanatics may plow through the five leisurely volumes of Edel's full-length biography of the master of American prose fiction; the rest of us can get the highlights in this single-volume version, condensed by Edel himself. (It also happens to be a bit franker about James's sexuality, always a juicy topic.) Edel's years of immersion pay off in intimate knowledge of a deeply fascinating man's life.

***Parallel Lives*** by Phyllis Rose (318 pp.) This group portrait of five Victorian marriages (the John Ruskins, the Thomas Carlyles, the John Stuart Mills, the Charles Dickenses, the George Eliots) raises a host of thorny issues—the nature of power in a sexual relationship, the toll that genius takes on the private life, the sheer strangeness of what goes on behind the bedroom doors of the famous. Follow up by reading the books written by Rose's subjects in subsequent months.

***Oscar Wilde*** by Richard Ellmann (680 pp.) Surely one of the finest biographies of our time, this exhaustive treatment of Wilde's life is at once scholarly, immensely moving, and incredibly funny (lots of quotes of Wilde at his best). "Wilde is one of us," writes Ellmann—his wit, his outrageousness, his radical approach to language and social issues are almost shockingly contemporary. The question remains: Was any of Wilde's art as creative as his life?

***The Five of Hearts*** by Patricia O'Toole (459 pp.) This is a charming portrait of a group of distinguished American eccentrics at the turn of the century—the historian Henry Adams and his wife Clover (a talented photographer who died a suicide), Secretary of State John Hay and his wealthy wife Clara, and Clarence King, who did an early geological survey of the West. Great on gossip, friendship, and the peculiar atmosphere of Washington at the dawn of America's world power.

***A Common Life*** by David Laskin (460 pp.) We can't claim to be objective (since one of us wrote this book) but it's safe to say that this group biography of the friendships between Nathaniel Hawthorne and Herman Melville, Henry James and Edith Wharton, Katherine Anne Porter and Eudora Welty, and Robert Lowell and Elizabeth Bishop is a book group natural. The book takes a thematic approach, focusing on how each pair navigated the cross currents between art and life. And it offers scores of ideas for future reading.

## Memoirs

***West with the Night*** by Beryl Markham (293 pp.) A pioneering pilot in colonial Africa, Markham lived a life of daring adventure back when most women couldn't even vote. Literary scandalmongers spread the rumor that Markham didn't write the book herself, but "dictated" it to her husband. Argue if you like about whose name should be on the cover; it's still a fascinating look at a woman—and an era—of a distinctly different stamp.

*Out of Africa* by Isak Dinesen (462 pp.) The Meryl Streep movie had glorious cinematography on its side, but read the book if you really want the nitty-gritty about Dinesen's years on a Kenyan coffee plantation: dealing with the natives, struggling to make ends meet, learning finally to love this strange and wonderful land. Fun to read in conjunction with *West with the Night;* Dinesen is a hundred times the better writer.

*In My Father's Court* by Isaac Bashevis Singer (307 pp.) Singer's memoir of his childhood in Warsaw's Jewish ghetto supplies a wonderful key to his fiction. As he eavesdrops on the bizarre people who visit his father, a widely respected Hasidic rabbi, for advice and justice, one sees how his imagination became schooled to marvels and troubles. It's also a vivid portrait of the customs and superstitions of a vanished world.

*Speak Memory* by Vladimir Nabokov (316 pp.) Nabokov grew up in a world of Tolstoyan splendor—vast country estates and pink granite palaces in St. Petersburg, with armies of servants—only to lose it all in the Revolution. The break between past and present resonates quietly in his fiction; here he deals with it directly, with lucid nostalgia. The recent Brian Boyd biography will help you determine where fact leaves off and playful Nabokovian fancy begins.

*Memories of a Catholic Girlhood* by Mary McCarthy (245 pp.) McCarthy's childhood, as recounted here, is as harrowing as fiction—the deaths of both her parents in the 1918 influenza epidemic, her exotic Jewish grandmother in Seattle, her cruel child-beating great-uncle. Then, when you read *Writing Dangerously,* Carol Brightman's recent biography of

McCarthy, you discover that a lot of this *is* fiction. Why was McCarthy compelled to fabricate?

**Good-bye to All That** by Robert Graves (347 pp.) In this memoir ("my bitter leave-taking of England," as Graves calls it), he writes as nakedly as he can of being thrust from the competitive, sports-obsessed homosexuality of an Edwardian boarding school into the horror of the trenches in World War I. This is definitely a young man's book, bent on breaking all the rules and spitting in the eye of authority.

**One Writer's Beginnings** by Eudora Welty (114 pp.) Welty presents her early life in Jackson, Mississippi, as a series of engrossing stories—about her parents' happy life, shattered by her father's early death; about parades, eccentric school teachers, and family trips north. It's curiously free of anger, sexuality, or the frustration that *any* brilliant woman must feel at spending a life at home with her mother—is she hiding something, or is she just supremely contented?

**Haywire** by Brooke Hayward (368 pp.) The author's mother, Margaret Sullavan, was a beautiful, gifted actress who died a bitter suicide. Her father, the legendary Hollywood agent Leland Hayward, made and lost millions, married five times, and alienated all his children. Brooke Hayward survived the wreckage to write this beautiful, thoughtful, absolutely riveting memoir—it towers over the "Mommie Dearest" school. Why hasn't she written anything else?

**Battlefield** by Peter Svenson (246 pp.) Svenson, an artist and would-be farmer, set out to buy his piece of paradise deep in the Virginia countryside and escape contemporary civilization. Then he discovered that he owned the field where the Battle of Cross Keys, an important and bloody Confederate victory early in the war, had been fought in 1862. Part memoir, part

Civil War history, part farm journal, part meditation on modern life, this volume opens out on any number of topics.

**An American Childhood** by Annie Dillard (255 pp.) One of America's most deft prose stylists, Dillard makes her 1950s girlhood in Pittsburgh seem magically unique and at the same time wonderfully familiar. With astonishing sensory memory, she somehow recreates the very texture of her life as a child—and, through that, teaches us how an individual begins to make sense of his or her environment. Reminiscences are bound to flow.

## Historical Fiction

**The French Lieutenant's Woman,** by John Fowles (366 pp.) Set in Victorian times, it combines the haunting sexiness of Thomas Hardy with a Dickensian mystery plot, spiced with references to Darwin and modern sexual mores. And its ingenious gimmick—two different endings from which to choose—is perfect for sparking reading group discussions.

**The Quincunx** by Charles Palliser (788 pp.) Critics compared this new twist on the Victorian novel to Dickens, Wilkie Collins, and Henry James, making liberal use of the term "tour de force." Palliser sets his complicated story of dispossession and intrigue in the violent underworld of late Regency London, tossing in puzzles involving the five-part figure of the quincunx. It's ingenious and gripping—but, in the end, is it merely clever?

**Possession: A Romance** by A. S. Byatt (555 pp.) Two counterpointed plots: one about two modern-day English academics, the other about the Victorian poets (à la Robert Browning and Christina Rossetti) whose secret lives they are unearthing.

Long strands of surprisingly good pseudo-Victorian poetry are thrown in for good measure. It's a long read, but a rewarding one, though group members may be sharply divided.

***The Volcano Lover*** by Susan Sontag (419 pp.) The love story of Admiral Nelson and Emma Hamilton, told from the point of view of her elderly intellectual husband, should have been more absorbing than it is here (the movie *That Hamilton Woman,* with Vivien Leigh and Laurence Olivier, told it better)—the bare facts alone are better than anything a supermarket tabloid could invent. The novel's oddness should provoke lively discussion, even if everyone agrees that it doesn't quite succeed as fiction.

***Memoirs of Hadrian*** by Marguerite Yourcenar (347 pp.) The first woman elected to France's elite Academie, Yourcenar exhaustively researched the life of this Roman emperor, then somehow managed to imagine herself into Hadrian's skin. The chiseled stateliness of classical Rome is combined with a powerful undercurrent of very real emotion in this unforgettable portrait of a historical figure.

***The Persian Boy*** by Mary Renault (419 pp.) A lower-brow version of *Memoirs of Hadrian,* this novel describes the court of Alexander the Great through the eyes of the slave boy who was his lover. Strong on historical detail, it's also a very readable yarn with sympathetic characters—good for groups who are more interested in content than in literary style.

***The Name of the Rose*** by Umberto Eco (612 pp.) A pretty unlikely combination—a mystery set in a medieval monastery, written by an Italian professor of semiotics. But the plot is almost good enough to satisfy detective-novel aficionados, and Eco's digressions about history and philosophy elevate it above pulp fiction. Though long, it's pretty readable. Good opening question: After all the fuss, is it really literature?

***Silence*** by Shusaku Endo (294 pp.) Endo, a Japanese Catholic who writes about East-West cultural clashes and Christianity, is quite accessible to Americans. This 1969 novel, perhaps his best, follows an idealistic fifteenth-century Portuguese Jesuit on a mission to Christianize Japan. In clear, slightly courtly prose he tells of a *Heart of Darkness*-like voyage to self-knowledge and recognition of The Other. Reading it is like living in another time and place—quietly spellbinding.

***Master and Commander*** by Patrick O'Brian (412 pp.) The first in a series of historical novels about British naval officer Jack Aubrey and ship doctor Stephen Maturin, this is set on a man o'war in Admiral Nelson's fleet during the Napoleonic Wars. Addicts of this series—quite a cult—rave about the fascinating technical ship detail, vivid dialogue, seafaring action, and strong character delineation.

***The English Patient*** by Michael Ondaatje (302 pp.) In a half-ruined Tuscan villa, April 1945, four survivors await the imminent end of World War II: a Canadian nurse, the severely burned pilot she tends, a maimed thief, and a Punjabi bomb-disposal expert. Brooding, atmospheric, and lushly written (the author is also a poet), it's a book of many-layered mysteries. To probe its heart, ask: Is this really a book about the war?

## Read the Book, See the Movie

***The Unbearable Lightness of Being*** by Milan Kundera (314 pp.) A trio of lovers in Prague, before, after, and during the 1968 uprising. Considering its setting, its epistemological ruminations, and its fragmented storytelling structure, this book should have been heavy going. Instead it's a joyous, moving, nostalgic, and very sexy read. Try to read it before seeing the excellent, faithful, but straightforward 1988 film version.

***Schindler's List*** by Thomas Keneally (397 pp.) From extensive interviews with fifty of the Holocaust survivors who owed their escape to German industrialist Oskar Schindler, Keneally created this novel of Schindler's incredibly courageous humanitarian scheme. Scrupulously true to the facts, the story itself is mind-blowing, but spare some attention to marvel at how well Keneally brings to life a man and an era he never knew personally.

***Damage*** by Josephine Hart (218 pp.) Told by a distinguished English physician and MP who destroys his life for love of his son's fiancée, this tensely poised, slim novel examines the destructive nature of passion. After viewing the gravely erotic film version, you may want to discuss which conveys the lovers' obsessive ardor better. Are they sympathetic in either one?

***Wide Sargasso Sea*** by Jean Rhys (190 pp.) This lushly written novel illuminates the Caribbean girlhood of the woman who married Edward Rochester, of *Jane Eyre* fame, and later went mad in his attic in England. But you don't have to have read the Brontë novel to enjoy this mesmerizing story—you just have to fall under its dreamy spell, a meditation on womanhood and, peripherally, on madness.

***Frankenstein*** by Mary Shelley (various editions; Penguin edition, 261 pp.) This celebrated tale of horror makes great reading—it's far stranger and more disturbing than the numerous film versions. But it's even more fascinating when you imagine Mary Shelley as she wrote this: nineteen years old, plunged in misery during a wet, cold summer in Switzerland with Percy Bysshe after their scandalous elopement.

***A Passage to India*** by E. M. Forster (362 pp.) Adela Quested visits Chandrapore, a provincial city in colonial India, and discovers that there's more to heaven and earth than was dreamt of in her philosophy back home in England. Forster's

willingness to leave spiritual mystery unsolved gives reso-
nance to what would otherwise be a gentle comedy of the Raj
era. The film is pretty and faithful, but does it do justice to the
book's riddling depths?

**The Sheltering Sky** by Paul Bowles (335 pp.) Talk about depressing. The writing is gorgeous and the north African desert
milieu is stunningly drawn, but the main characters—a trio of
expatriate Americans—are selfish, doomed wretches. Some
people love this book, others hate it, and no one feels
neutral—it's bound to provoke discussion.

# There's an epidemic with 27 million victims. And no visible symptoms.

It's an epidemic of people who can't read.

Believe it *or* not, 27 million Americans are functionally illiterate, about one adult in five.

The solution to this problem is you… when you join the fight against illiteracy. So call the Coalition for Literacy at toll-free 1-800-228-8813 and volunteer.

## Volunteer Against Illiteracy. The only degree you need is a degree of caring.